Grief Is Not Forever

Grief Is Not Forever

Jeri Krumroy

Foreword by Clyde M. Narramore

BRETHREN PRESS
Elgin, Illinois

Grief Is Not Forever

BRETHREN PRESS, 1451 Dundee Avenue, Elgin, IL 60120

Cover design by Kathy Kline
Scripture quotations are from the New American Standard Bible, © The Lockman Foundation 1960, 1962, 1963, 1968, 1971, 1972, 1973, 1975, 1977, unless otherwise noted.

Library of Congress Cataloging in Publication Data

Krumroy, Jeri, 1925
    Grief is not forever.

    1. Krumroy, Jeri, 1925-   2. Krumroy, Dick. 3. Christian biography—United States. 4. Multiple myeloma—Biography. 5. Breavement—Religious aspects—Christianity. I. Title.
BR1700.2.K78   1985   248.8'6'0922   [B]   85-24256
ISBN 0-87178-326-6

Printed in the United States of America

Dedicated to

my counselor and personal friend,
Dr. Maurice Wagner, who promised,
"I'll stick with you the best I can"
when I faced the
greatest ordeal of my life.
With his constant support and guidance
before and after I said goodbye, I was
able to let God heal my broken heart
and move me from grief into
life with a purpose.

Acknowledgements

I wish to express my heartfelt appreciation to Dr. Clyde Narramore and Dr. Maurice Wagner for their friendship and support during my long ordeal, and for their encouragement while writing this book. To my many friends at the Narramore Foundation and elsewhere who caringly prayed for Dick and me and encouraged us while we suffered, many thanks. My friend Karen Ann Wojahn deserves special mention. She spent countless hours typing, editing, and evaluating my material, served faithfully as my advocate, and encouraged me not to give up. Although the names of most people in this book have been changed to protect their privacy, I owe them my gratitude for the part they have played in my life.

Contents

Foreword

When I invited Dick and Jeri Krumroy to join the staff of the Narramore Christian Foundation, I did so with my eyes wide open. It happened like this.

One day a few years back I received a letter from Dick saying that he had cancer and that his doctors in Akron, Ohio, had given him about two years to live. Dick wanted to move to California so that he and Jeri could join our staff. "Then," he said, "when I go home to be with the Lord, Jeri will be among friends at the Narramore Christian Foundation. This way she will be much happier . . . and I will, too."

I invited Dick and Jeri to our New Year's Conference on campus. During that time we could make a mutual decision. They arrived soon afterward, and we had a great week together. I saw how outstanding a couple they were and invited them to join our staff.

"Do you know, Dr. Narramore, what you are getting yourself into?" Dick asked cautiously.

We talked frankly about the probability of his getting worse and worse, his hospitalization, and eventual death. I assured him that I understood pretty well what was likely to come, but that our Foundation believes *every person is worth understanding.*

"We help people all over the world," I reassured, "and we want to help you. Go back to Akron, take care of the loose ends, and come back to Rosemead as soon as you can. You're part of the family!"

What happened after they made the move is told in this excellent book by Jeri. My decision to include them in our Foundation family was one of the best decisions I have ever made. I'm sure you'll understand why long before you reach the last chapter in this tremendous book!

I've watched Jeri not only deal with her grief, but change and grow and become a strong, beautiful person. It is one thing to get help for one's own problems but it is another to pass what one has learned to others.

Jeri has learned not only to "stand," but to reach out and be a source of strength and blessing to others. Calls come on a regular basis for her to minister to church groups and others around the country. She remains a valued member of our staff as she lectures to the scores of hurting people who attend our seminars at Rosemead.

One of the things that has been most helpful has been the teaching of practical ways the church can minister to those who are experiencing grief and loss. We've seen these ideas put to the test, and they work!

Someone has said, "in order to practice love, we must become vulnerable." This book is a labor of love. Jeri has made herself vulnerable in writing it. It will be a lamp in the tunnel of grief. It will be a light to point the way to wholeness, joy and service.

Truly we have seen the Lord . . . "give beauty for ashes, the oil of joy for mourning, the garment of praise for the spirit of heaviness . . . " God indeed has been "glorified."

Dr. Clyde M. Narramore
Narramore Christian Foundation

1

"Why This, Why Now?"

"We . . . I have a final diagnosis, Mrs. Krumroy."

Our doctor's voice could not conceal his struggle for words. He sounded strangely subdued, and I felt a flicker of fear. Standing amid half-packed moving crates, I gripped the telephone receiver a little tighter and took a long, deep breath. "What is it?" I asked.

"It's called multiple myeloma, Mrs. Krumroy. It's cancer of the bone marrow. I'm sorry."

"Sorry?" I was puzzled. "Can't you treat it?" I asked. Silence. When the doctor didn't answer, I nodded. "How long will he live?"

"Maybe two years, or less . I'm sorry," he said again.

In a far-away voice that sounded unfamiliar, I heard myself thank him. Mechanically I replaced the telephone receiver. In those few seconds my life was changed, forever. My husband, Dick, had taken an early retirement, and we had purchased a lot in Florida where we were planning to build a new home. Our house was on the market and I was in the middle of packing. Now, everything was changed.

"Jeri, are you all right?" My friend Nancy stood beside me. I'd forgotten she was there to help me pack.

"Nancy," I murmured, "Dick has cancer. The doctor says he's going to die." I began to tremble. "Why? Why this? *Why now?*" I cried.

Without a word, Nancy put her arms around me, and we stood sobbing together. She had lost her son only recently in the Vietnam war, and she knew that words were futile against the pain I was experiencing.

That evening in the hospital, Dick and I sat staring at each other. Tears blurred our eyes. *God, I agonized, you can't take away the person I love above all else in this world. How can I face life without him? How can I watch him suf-*

fer? What possible good can come from all this? I'll never make it on my own.

"Multiple myeloma. It sounds kind of pretty, doesn't it?" Dick finally broke the awkward silence. Then his voice dropped to a whisper, and he stared out the window. "It isn't so pretty, though."

I didn't know what to say. Dick had always led our conversations. I wanted to be brave and hopeful for him, but to speak would only betray my rising panic.

"Jeri." Dick's voice was calm and reassuring. He took my hand. "I've tried to show my friends and family how to live as a Christian. Now I'll try to show them how to die."

His words cut deeply. I could barely see him through my tears. *That's no comfort,* I thought. *How can anyone be brave in the face of such sorrow!* Suddenly the tears were spilling. Dick reached out to me, and we held each other and cried.

Driving home from the hospital that night I kept thinking, *but two years is so short!* I realized for the first time how brief life really is. Our children were grown, and it seemed to me that this ought to be our season of serenity— a time to grow old together gracefully. Now our dream was shattered . . . Not at all the "happily ever after" life I'd fantasized just twenty-five years ago. . . .

It was March, I remember, but spring hadn't arrived yet in Ohio. World War II had been over for a little more than a year, and my girlfriend, Millie, wanted me to meet "Mr. Right."

"Dick Krumroy is his name, and you *have* to meet him!" Millie giggled. "He's tall and handsome! If you marry him, it will be my *third* successful match-making!"

"Oh, Millie!" I answered. "You can't play cupid all the time. You know it's only been two weeks since I broke my engagement. I need time . . . besides, it's snowing, and I have to wash my hair."

But Millie was persistent. My excuses weakened and I went to her house after all. I removed my snowboots in the kitchen and stepped into the living room. Then I saw him.

At that moment, Dick Krumroy looked more like a big green giant than prince charming. Dressed in a dark green pinstriped suit, Dick's six foot, two inch frame towered well above me. I looked up and smiled.

When he drove me home that night, we talked. He told me about his construction business and his plans for his future as a builder. I was impressed with his kindness and his gentleness. He seemed eager to be protective, carefully holding my arm as we walked so I wouldn't slip on the ice.

The next night he took me out to dinner at a quaint little French cafe with white linen tablecloths and linen napkins. We talked for hours over the flickering candlelight, and it seemed as though we had known each other forever. We discussed the kind of home we wanted and how many children we would like to have when we eventually found the "right" person to marry.

The snow was falling softly when we left the restaurant, and we could feel it crunching beneath our feet as we made our way to Dick's car. Carefully he guided my steps and made sure I was safe inside the car before going around to his side. I felt completely secure and and at ease with him.

Once inside the car, Dick gazed at me affectionately. Suddenly he leaned over and kissed me tenderly. "Do you believe in love at first sight, Jeri?" he asked.

"I . . . I'm not sure." My face suddenly felt flushed. "Do you?"

"Yes, I do. Will you marry me?"

I was shocked. Only two days had passed! Although I really did not believe in love at first sight, I *did* have a sense of peace about Dick. He was direct and open and sure of himself—qualities that contrasted sharply with my own less-confident personality.

"Ah . . . well, I have to think, Dick," I stammered. "Things are moving too fast!"

But I didn't think for very long. Later that night I told my mother Dick was the man I wanted to marry.

"Jeri," Mom frowned. "You've only just broken up

with your young sailor. Are you sure you don't want to marry Dick on the rebound?"

"I don't know," I said, "but—"

"Are you really in love with him?"

"I'm not desperately in love, no." I felt angry. "But he's the one I want to spend the rest of my life with. I'm twenty-three, Mom. This is no school-girl crush."

I don't know why I felt so soon that Dick was the right choice, but there was an overwhelming peace about my decision.

I said yes to Dick the evening after his proposal, and we lost no time in planning our wedding. The night before we married, I kept watch beneath a moonlit window, counting the flickering stars. I talked to God about my wedding and the lifetime we would share. It was a strange thing for me to be really sure about anything, but I was certain about this. Marrying Dick was right.

The wedding was on a sun-burnished June day. My gown was trimmed with beads and trained with tulle. The bridesmaids wore delicate pink, and my maid of honor was gowned in blue. Three hundred guests had filled the cathedral-type church, and I marched proudly down the aisle on my father's arm.

Dick stood confidently at the front waiting for me. If he was nervous in his role as a bridegroom, no one would have guessed. He wore a blue-grey suit. *How handsome he is!* I thought. Then, for a fleeting moment, I felt irritated with him. *Why doesn't he look at me?* I wondered as I swept grandly toward the altar.

Later he explained that the woman who catered the wedding had told him that it "wasn't the thing to do" to look at the bride as she came toward him! It still surprises me that he would take a woman's advice so readily.

Dick almost pulled me back down the aisle after the ceremony, he was so excited. We had a joyous reception, complete with three-tiered wedding cake. We posed patiently for photographs, then whisked away for a storybook honeymoon.

The happy days of early marriage went swiftly by and, within a couple of years, our beautiful children, Janie and Bobby, came along. Life wasn't perfect—it never is. Yet I was content, all my girlhood dreams seemed to be coming true. I was secure, well-cared for, and the blissful, contented mother I'd always wanted to be. The children gave me hours of joy, and Dick provided everything we could want. His construction business was successful, and our home lacked nothing. I sometimes wondered, though, *Where would I be without Dick? He's the source of all my security.* Was something missing?

Dick and I had come from different church backgrounds, although as young adults our faith had been rather nominal. After settling into married life, we found a nearby church and attended regularly. Dick even taught an adult Sunday School class. Then one evening a group of us went to hear a noted evangelist who had come to Akron. He was a warm, vibrant speaker, who seemed to know God in a personal way and I kept thinking how nice it would be to know God personally too. One of the vivid things I remember about this distinguished preacher's sermon was his confession, "I deserve nothing less than Hell!"

I almost fell off my seat. *If this man thinks he deserves Hell, what makes me think I deserve otherwise?* The question haunted me for weeks, although I had no doubt I was living a Christian life. Yet I had no solid assurance for that belief, other than my own basic sense of morality.

One sunny morning shortly thereafter I found myself sitting in my kitchen, sipping coffee with a close friend. "Jeri, there's a Bible study in my neighborhood that's really fantastic. I'd love to have you come with me," she invited.

Curious, I inquired "when does it meet?"

"Tonight at seven-thirty. I'll come by and pick you up."

"No, no. I just couldn't—not tonight," I protested. "Dick will be home and . . . ."

"You'll love the teacher, Jeri, and—"

After running out of excuses, I finally gave in to her

persistence and agreed to go. As evening drew closer, however, I became more and more anxious about going to this Bible study. I'd never left my family in the evening before unless I cleared it first with Dick. He surprised me by his willingness for me to go.

The speaker seemed like a talking Bible! Never before had I remembered hearing anything like what he had to say. He explained about having a secure relationship with God. Questions were fielded easily. He seemed at home in both the Old and New Testaments, quoting the Scriptures as though they were truly relevant for today. Two well known verses captured my ear:

> For God sent not his Son into the world to condemn the world; but that the world through him might be saved . . . for there is none other name under heaven given among men, whereby we must be saved.
>
> John 3:17; Acts 4:12 (KJV)

After the class, I made my way to the teacher, a local pastor, and asked to speak with him.

"Could you please tell me what it *means* to be saved?"

He smiled warmly. "Would you mind if I came to your house some evening? I'd like to share the meaning of salvation with both you and your husband."

"Can you come Saturday?"

"Of course."

This was something new. I'd never asked anyone to our home without Dick's approval, but I sensed this visit was important. Of course, I waited until Saturday to tell him. When supper was almost over, I said, "Dick, the Bible study leader, pastor Felton, is coming over tonight."

"What is *he* coming over for?"

"He's coming to tell us what it means to be saved," I explained.

Dick sighed impatiently. "Jeri, we go to a fine church, and I teach Sunday School. We live clean, moral lives. Besides—that man is a fanatic!"

You're probably right, I thought. *You always are. But I*

really want to know about this.

Dick received our guest warmly in spite of his feelings. He didn't even seem too upset when pastor Felton quoted Romans 3:23, "For all have sinned and fallen short of the glory of God." But the more he talked, the more Dick argued. Finally, Rev. Felton became exasperated.

"All right, then, Dick. You seem quite self-sufficient. But on exactly what *do* you base your salvation?" He closed his Bible, said goodnight, and left.

This question brewed in Dick's brain for several days, then one night he announced his decision that we needed to take some classes at the Akron Bible Institute with which pastor Felton was associated. For the next several months we took weekly classes. The first hour we studied the book of James, the second hour we attended chapel, and the third hour we took a class in "How to Give Your Faith Away."

Christ came into our lives in a new way. We felt renewed, whole, and at peace. Week after week I responded to the invitation to receive Christ as my personal Savior, but as my faith matured, and as I studied more and more of James, I realized I needed to thank God for my salvation. I didn't have to keep asking God to save me.

One thing did trouble me. All around me were Christians who had much to offer God in the way of talents and gifts. Dick was an excellent businessman, and after he recommitted his life to Christ, he was asked to serve on the board of the Akron Bible Institute. But I had no visible talent—nothing to offer God.

Soon a friend asked me to attend a teacher-training class with Child Evangelism Fellowship. These teachers were being trained to share God's Love and the gospel with boys and girls in their own neighborhoods through Good News Clubs. Someone requested prayer for a home where club meetings could be held, and I volunteered our home for the classes.

During the weeks that followed, I discovered that I not only could exercise the gift of hospitality, but also that I had a flair for telling stories and keeping the attention of the children. When I heard a prayer request for another teacher, I responded, and in the years that followed, I helped other women open their homes. This led to the privilege of leading many women and children to a personal relationship with God through faith in Jesus Christ.

Meanwhile, another friend invited me to a Christian Women's Club luncheon, sponsored by the Christian Women's Club of America. This organization has a unique project of supporting rural and village missions in the United States and of reopening closed churches by sending them home missionaries. As Dick began to read about these missions-at-home, he encouraged me to participate in the clubs.

"Jeri," he pronounced one day, "I believe God is calling us to a new work!"

"What kind of work?" I asked, stunned.

"I have all these building skills. I can help construct churches all over rural America. When we finish one, we can move on to the next place. I've called an appraiser to give us an idea of what the house is worth. What do you think?"

My heart sank. I was happy where we were. Why did we need to move? What about Bobby and Janie? Was this best for them? Yet I was fearful of expressing my real feelings. I knew Dick had made a decision already, so I avoided a direct answer.

I mumbled something about having to finish preparing supper and strode into the kitchen. I was relieved that Dick didn't notice how upset I was.

For the next three days I prayed constantly, "Lord, if you want us to do this, then make me willing to walk away from our home with no regrets, and help me to be able to say goodbye." Within that time I sensed a peace that swelled over me again and again. God had answered my prayer.

By the following summer, the house was still unsold, and Christian Women's Club of America assigned us the task of building a small church in Moscow, Michigan. Instead of vacationing that summer, we loaded ourselves and the children into our station wagon every weekend and headed north. During the week, Dick would fly to New York where he was building a truck terminal. He somehow ran his own construction business even at this feverish pace. When the church in Moscow was completed and dedicated, papers were prepared for us that would officially document our acceptance into mission work.

Those papers were never signed. A week after the dedication, Dick awakened me abruptly in the middle of the night, his voice quavering.

"Jeri, call the coctor . . . it's my head. The pain is awful!"

After several days of exhausting examinations, the diagnosis was revealed. Dick had experienced a cerebral hemorrhage. To complicate matters, the extensive testing had left him paralyzed on one side. For three days he was unable to speak. His doctors warned that he would probably never walk or work again.

Having prayed with childlike faith for opportunities to serve God, we were now faced with an unthinkable calamity. How was I supposed to raise two children under twelve without a father? Dick was the unchallenged, absolute leader of our family. The thought of being in charge, making decisions, and functioning without him was absurd. I felt incompetent, incapable of handling such responsibility. Although I understood that God is the source of my security, Dick was so much more tangible!

I struggled daily to put Dick's health in God's hands. Now as he lay paralyzed in the hospital, I prayed for strength to accept whatever God had for me. Alone in my quiet kitchen one night, Bible in hand, I did something that is seldom wise to do—I allowed the book to simply fall open, hoping for a word of comfort. The breathtaking words of a Psalm leaped off the page and made their home in my heart.

I love the Lord, because he hears my voice and
my supplications.

Because he has inclined his ear to me, therefore I
shall call upon him as long as I live . . .

Return to your rest, O my soul, for the Lord has
dealt bountifully with you.

For thou hast rescued my soul from death, my
eyes from tears, my feet from stumbling. I shall walk
before the Lord in the land of the living.

Psalm 116:1, 2, 7–9

Ecstatically, I took this as God's assurance that Dick
would live, that better days were ahead! Even when Dick's
condition worsened temporarily a few days later, I knew
the Lord would not forsake me in crisis.

After six weeks in the hospital, Dick lifted his leg about
a half inch off the bed. He let out a whoop of excitement
that brought the nurses running from the other end of the
hall.

"I have hope now, Jeri," he laughed. "I asked the Lord
to heal me, and that I see Bobby and Janie through school,
and maybe married. Then I'll be ready to go."

Gradually Dick was able to move his legs a little more,
progressing from a wheelchair to a walker. In seven long
weeks he improved enough to move to a rehabilitation
center. After three months of therapy at the center, he was
able to come home using a walker. Finally, he walked on
his own again. What joy and gratefulness filled my heart
when he stood by my side once more!

Dick's recuperation at home was a traumatic time. We
were developing a new perspective on life—taking it one
day at a time. We were also beginning to experience a difference in our husband and wife roles. Because Dick was
unable to do a lot of things for himself, I discovered for the
first time that he needed me as much as I needed him. I
longed for the days when Dick could resume his duty as my
protector.

In the Old Testament Job became our constant friend
as we studied the Bible together. We admired his strong

faith in God—faith that allowed him to say, "Though he slay me, I will hope in Him" (Job 13:15). Once we read Hebrews 12:6 together: "For those whom the Lord loves He disciplines, and He scourges every son whom He receives."

Dick chuckled a little sadly. "Sometimes I almost wish God didn't love me quite as much, Jeri!"

Often I told Dick, "Honey, if anything ever happens to you, I want to use my life for Jesus. Perhaps I could work with some kind of Christian ministry."

As the days turning into weeks grew into months, then dragged into five and finally ten years, the difficulties of Dick's health seemed to shrink my faith from the size of a healthy melon into a delicate mustard seed. I feared that I wouldn't be able to honor the Lord in all of my problems, and I chided myself for limited faith. The comfort of Scripture verses kept me steady. "By grace you have been saved through faith; and that not of yourselves, it is the gift of God; not as a result of works, that no one should boast" Ephesians 2:8–9).

These words were strength to me, because they helped me remember that having faith was not up to me! God would even take the responsibility for that. I simply had to ask, and greater faith would be there to sustain me.

Gradually Dick was able to establish a work routine. His business partner brought work to the house and, as the months went by, Dick was finally able to go back to work full time. Dick's sharing of his courage and faith in the face of his adversity helped many of his colleagues to faith in Christ.

As a homemaker, I found a ministry in my community through leading women's Bible studies. It had taken ten long years, but we seemed to be living a normal life at last. I was grateful that in all the months and years of Dick's recovery, I never had to handle his financial responsibilities or make any major decisions alone.

The children graduated from Christian colleges, and Bob fell in love with a wonderful young Christian woman. We were thrilled when Lonnie agreed to marry him. Janie had taken an apartment close to her teaching position and was preparing to marry Randy within the year. God had honored Dick's prayer, and I was almost afraid to think beyond that.

Our house was too big for us, though, and we had to start thinking of a smaller place. We talked about selling the house and moving to an apartment, or building on our property in Florida.

Suddenly, to our surprise, Dick's business partner announced that he wanted to buy Dick's portion of the company. After agonizing over this in prayer, Dick concluded that less work pressure and a move to Florida might be just the thing for his health. Within a matter of weeks, Dick sold the business.

I had a sad, sinking feeling inside as the "For Sale" sign went up in the front yard of the house we had shared for twenty-two years. Although resigned to the change, my feelings of apprehension began to grow. I felt threatened and uneasy. Something was wrong.

One day Dick was carrying some trash cans up from the basement when he doubled over in pain. "Jeri!" he cried, "Help me! I've pulled a muscle or something."

Dick's pain was more than a simple muscle strain, and hospitalized for the next week he was in agony as he lay in traction. I was frustrated and angry with him for not taking better care of himself.

Dick was not home from the hospital long when a young couple, prospective buyers, came to see the house. Dick's back hurt worse than ever, and he couldn't get off the couch. The couple wandered through and made an offer fair to all of us.

Two mornings after the house sold, Dick couldn't get out of bed. I phoned the doctor, and his words were firm.

"Call an ambulance right away, Mrs. Krumroy. Get Dick to the hospital."

2

"Okay, Lord, What Is It?"

The shock of Dick's diagnosis left me stunned. The intensity of his pain was due to a broken back! Because of cancer in the bone marrow, any jarring could result in fractures. Some of the vertebrae had broken, probably from the strain of lifting the trash cans.

For several days after the diagnosis I moved in a haze from room to room, packing and unpacking the same boxes. Faced with Dick's death sentence, I rushed back and forth to the hospital twice a day. The sixty-day deadline for moving out of our house came closer and, as that reality hit me, I almost panicked.

"I don't know how to do this, Dick," I said one afternoon at the hospital. "The doctor says you can't come home for several weeks. By that time we have to be out of the house. I'll have to find an apartment and move by myself."

"I've got it all figured out, Jeri." Dick sounded his usual confident self. "Fred and Kristine from church will help you find a suitable apartment—Fred knows the kinds of things to look for. You'll have to pay first and last month's rent. There's plenty of money in savings for that.

"The movers will take care of the major packing," he continued. "You can do the little stuff. Call the utilities and arrange to have them shut off the power at the house the day escrow closes. You already know when that is. You'll have to be at the apartment the day the utilities go on there. Bring the bills to the hospital. I'll take care of them."

Relief washed over me. Dick had thought of everything. Even so, I had to call the movers and make all the arrangements, and then Fred went with me to select an apartment. It was a lovely, brand new, two-bedroom apartment with two bathrooms. I had to pick out the wall paper by myself, and though I disliked doing it without Dick's input,

I finally settled on a bold yellow with orange poppies.

I set the day for the move and began sorting through all of our belongings to decide what we should keep. It was a monumental task. I had no idea how much one family of four can accumulate in twenty-two years. Even though Bob and Janie were grown and living on their own, we still had many of their things in the attic.

I called Janie and asked her to gather some friends to help bring everything down from the attic, but the task was still greater than I could handle. Finally I swallowed my pride and called on the women from the Bible study groups I had led for the last four years. They helped me sort and label everything in my home and I ran a garage sale ad in the newspaper.

One night I came home from visiting Dick at the hospital and went upstairs to bed. I had just dozed off when the phone rang. It was a man.

"Is your husband home?" he asked.

"No," I mumbled. "Dick's in the hospital. Can I take a message?"

"This is Chuck Burton from Nathum Corporation. When do you expect Dick out of the hospital?"

"Not for a few weeks," I answered, sleepily.

The phone clicked in my ear. *That's odd,* I thought. *He didn't even say goodbye.* I kept trying to remember if I'd ever heard the man's name before. Suddenly fear grabbed me. *I should never have let a stranger know I'm alone in the house.* I got up and double checked all of the doors and windows, making sure they were locked. The next day I asked Dick about the caller but he had never heard of him, or the company.

"I think you'd better ask Fred and Kristine to let you stay with them until you get moved," Dick said. "I don't want you at the house alone." I moved in with Fred and Kristine, and even during the day I tried to make sure there was someone with me whenever I was at the house. I didn't like being alone.

A few days later I had to make a decision, and it upset

me to have to make it alone. Because multiple myeloma causes the bones to become brittle, Dick's back would need extra support. Our mattress was too soft, and I worried about rolling over and disturbing him. I ordered twin beds with extra-firm mattresses, then asked Fred to go along with me to select a headboard that would join them together.

"What color do you think I should choose, Fred?"

"I don't know, Jeri," he shrugged, "It's your headboard."

"But what kind do you think Dick would like?"

"You know him better than I do, Jeri."

"Well, what kind of material should it be made of? Do you like the green and yellow one, or is the orange and gold one better?"

"Jeri, this is your decision. I can't decide what color you'd like, and I won't."

I felt a flash of anger, but quickly squashed it. Finally I selected the gold brushed-velvet headboard, even though I still felt uneasy about the decision.

"Fred, do you think Dick will like it? Do you think I've made a good choice?"

"I'm sure it will be fine," he sighed, and I'm certain he was relieved to drop me at home.

I still didn't realize how much I depended upon Dick and his approval in my decisions. Being unwilling to step out on my own, independently, was part of being a godly, submissive wife, wasn't it? It did occur to me, though, that when Dick was gone, I'd be lost without someone to help me.

God, I prayed, *are you big enough to pull this one off for me? If you're willing to see me through this nightmare, I'm willing to press on.*

The days were filled with so much activity that I really didn't have time to feel sorry for myself. Janie and Bob were both shaken by the news of their dad's illness, but I felt they were handling it as well as could be expected. We all had to keep on going, doing, living.

I started sorting things in the attic of the house and worked my way to the basement. One afternoon as I was going through a box of books, I came across some material written by Dr. Clyde Narramore, a Christian psychologist from California. His books had been helpful to me when I taught Bible studies for children and women, and I listened faithfully to his radio broadcasts.

Dick and I were impressed with Dr. Narramore's ministry because he was interested in the whole person. We had attended several conferences sponsored by the Narramore Christian Foundation because of Dr. Narramore's concern for salvation and spiritual growth as well as the mental, emotional and physical well-being of persons.

For the next several days, Dr. Narramore's name and the work of the Foundation continually came into my mind. At first I was irritated about this interruption to my thoughts, but finally I concluded that God was trying to tell me something. While cleaning out the cupboards in the basement, I spoke aloud. "Okay, God, what is it?" Instantly, words from Philippians 2:13 came to my mind: "It is God who is at work in you, both to will and to work for His good pleasure."

What did this verse from the Bible have to do with our grim future and the Narramore Foundation far away in California? Could God possibly use me in some way there after Dick's death?

"God! California is so far away from Bob and Janie," I argued. "And don't you know we own property in Florida?"

I found myself wandering into the family room, flooded by memories of the smiling faces of countless neighborhood children. So many of them had learned about Jesus there. Upstairs, in our warmly-decorated living room, God had used me as an instrument to teach women the wonders of the Bible. After Dick and I had committed our lives to Christ, we had dedicated our home to God. We used it for Christian service.

Tears blurred my eyes. "God," I whispered, "If California is where you want me to go, I'm willing."

I felt alone until a warm sense of closeness to a loving Father surrounded me. I vowed that I wouldn't breathe a word of my conversation with God to any one.

My mother-in-law had spent much of that day keeping Dick company in his hospital room while I packed, but she had left just before I arrived that evening. I hadn't crossed the short distance between the door and Dick's bedside before he lifted his head from the pillow and grinned.

"Jeri, how would you like to go visit the Narramore Christian Foundation after I get on my feet again?"

I caught my breath. *Holy Spirit, you certainly have it all over Alexander Graham Bell!* I thought. Dick settled back onto the pillow as I approached the bed.

"Whatever made you say that?" I smiled, although I was fighting tears. I knew the Holy Spirit had spoken to both of us.

"I've been thinking all day about us. You've said so many times that if something happened to me, you'd want to serve God in a Christian organization. Wouldn't you like me to go with you?"

Awed by the miracle that had occurred in our lives, I managed to respond, "Of course I would!" Inside, I wondered how in the world we would ever get to California, much less live there, with Dick's physical limitations. But then again, Dick's business had been successful. We had some savings and adequate insurance to cover his medical needs. There was no doubt in my mind though that God was leading us.

"They might even be able to put me to work, too." Dick smiled wistfully as he took my hand. I never doubted they could use Dick—but what could they do with me?

I wrote to the Foundation, explaining our situation, and they responded with cards and letters of encouragement. Finally, six weeks after Dick entered the hospital, he was released. We went directly to our new apartment. Dick never went back to our old house again.

During those weeks of hospitalization, Dick had decided to change banks, and I had to have a new identification photo taken. I had no idea of the toll that had been taken on me personally until I saw the photo. Dark circles under my eyes and worry lines across my forehead made me look a troubled fifteen years older.

"Jeri! This picture is terrible!" Dick exclaimed when he saw it. "You go right back down to the bank and tell them your husband wants them to take a new picture!"

A few months later, after asking about possible service opportunities with the Narramore Christian Foundation, a letter arrived. A conference was planned for after Christmas, and we were invited to attend. Fortunately, it would be held during a week when Dick wasn't having chemotherapy. We decided to go. I was so numb I wasn't even aware of when the plane took off or landed.

As the conference progressed, Dick and I both sensed God's presence. We also felt ourselves on the edge of a great decision. After a day of psychological testing and a full week of lectures and group sessions, I sat in our motel room reading the Bible and praying. Years before, as a new Christian, I had been given I Corinthians 14:33 as a formula for God's will: "For God is not the author of confusion, but of peace . . . ."

"Lord," I prayed, "if you want me to make a major move like this, leaving my dearest friends and coming out here to a strange place with my dying husband, you will have to fill me with peace."

This assurance came to me the night before we were to leave California. Dick and I were walking up a lane to our motel when suddenly a warm, peaceful feeling flowed through me. I knew for certain that we were meant to work for the Foundation. I heard God's voice clearly, "this is it." At that point, however, I said nothing to Dick.

The next morning, Dr. Narramore called us into his office to review our psychological tests. "I see nothing negative here," he mused, pointing to our test results. Then he smiled, "We would be proud to have you on our staff. We could use your business expertise, Dick, in the accounting office. And Jeri, you'd be most helpful as a coordinator for our Discovery Day program. Would you be willing to come?"

"Do you know what you're getting into?" Dick asked cautiously.

"Yes, Dick, I do. Your cancer may worsen. You may have to spend time in the hospital. There'll be days when the pain will keep you from being able to work. Eventually, you may go home to be with God in Eternity. But Dick, we here at the Foundation believe that every person is worth understanding. We want to help you."

Dick turned to me with a penetrating gaze. He spoke gently. "Well, I'm ready to come. Now we'll have to convince Jeri."

I shook my head. "No, Dick, God's already done the convincing. The Lord has given me the peace I've asked for. I'm ready to come, too."

"Fine!" beamed Dr. Narramore. "Now go back to Akron, take care of the loose ends, and come back to Rosemead as soon as you can. You're part of the family!"

So it was that we did the unthinkable. We pulled up our deep, dear roots in the midst of tragedy and overwhelming sorrow, and we followed God's leading.

The next weeks were emotion-filled with tears and heart-rending goodbyes. Our children had both moved to other states, but they came home for Christmas. While we were excited to see them, our joy was lessened by sorrow. Would this be our last holiday together?

Almost as difficult as having to face that possibility was having to say goodbye to near lifelong friends from our local church. Yet underneath was a constant, underlying peace. Somehow, deep within us, we knew that God was preparing us for the ordeal to come. We didn't realize just how intense the trial would be, but we knew the Creator's hand was upon us, placing us in the midst of caring people who were prepared to help us while we helped others.

The morning we were scheduled to leave, we got up early and made coffee to take with us. We had packed everything else the day before, so I loaded the car with the last-minute items. A radio weather report announced a coming snowstorm. The sky was dark as we started out with Dick behind the wheel. Turning around to look out the rear window as we drove out of the city, I whispered, "Goodbye, Akron!" *How perfect your timing is, God. Eleven years ago I asked you to help me to be willing to leave my home and go into a ministry, and then you gave me all this time to get used to the idea. And I am ready now. I really am.*

Even such a sense of peace did not diminish the feeling of loss. The further we drove, the harder it snowed. Then we hit an ice storm. Bleak weather added to my deep sense of grief—leaving friends and family and facing the possibility of my husband's death. There were many times during that trip when sunglasses hid my tears from Dick.

When we reached Rosemead we discovered that the Foundation was providing us with a newly acquired rental home, complete with a swimming pool. Since the house was adjacent to the facilities, we could walk back and forth, and I'd be able to go home to care for Dick on the days when he was too sick to come to work. I would never have to be alone when he was in the hospital either.

The house, unfortunately, was in poor condition. It needed to be cleaned and painted, but it was a perfect little cottage for us. Dick hired someone to put a gate from the backyard to the Narramore property. Our small house became bright and airy with a new coat of paint. Dick and I had fun making small repairs and buying new furniture. Soon we had a cheery, comfortable home of which we could be proud.

The world-famous City of Hope cancer research center was just forty-five minutes away. It was better equipped than virtually any other hospital for handling the severity of Dick's illness. It seemed to us to be the right place for him.

Dick scheduled an appointment with the chief surgeon and showed him his X-rays. The doctor shook is head. "You have multiple myeloma. That's one kind of cancer we don't service." Then he added, "But if you feel you were called out here, let's let God worry about your health." Soon

Dick's application for therapy was accepted. We both knew that we had been led through a new door, and that knowledge was exhilarating. I was gripped, though, with a numb feeling most of the time. The stark reality that I was losing my husband was always before me.

My psychological test had revealed that I was more depressed than normal even though I felt compelled to hide my feelings behind a cheerful smile and to give just the "right" or vague answers to people concerned about Dick's illness. I was angry, apprehensive, and crying inside. How *could* I live the rest of my life without Dick? He had faced the world for me all of these years.

I sensed a strange irony in this. We had traveled thousands of miles to share in a ministry of aid to others. Yet I was growing more and more aware of my own need. Why had God led me into such a confusing dilemma? It wasn't long before I began to see that God *was* at work within me, and that this work had only just begun.

3
Grief—Already?

"How does this look, Jeri?" Dick stood before me dressed in a new suit. He'd lost weight, but these clothes fit him perfectly.

"You look *terrific,* honey!" I grinned. We were going to a dinner party with some people at the Foundation, and I was looking forward to a relaxing evening. Dick's pain had steadily worsened, and he'd been in and out of City of Hope several times in the six months since our move. It was encouraging that he felt well enough to go out.

Our special efforts to make him look nice that night were successful. Dick looked well. Unless a person had seen a portrait of him in healthy years, they would not suspect how sick my husband really was. Although our new friends knew about Dick's illness, he looked well, and he minimized his discomfort when they asked about it.

This intensified my own feelings of sadness. *How can anyone imagine what I'm going through with Dick at home?* Dick was finding most movement terribly painful. It was difficult for him, even, to embrace me. I desperately missed the bear hugs he used to give.

But tonight he felt better, and I was grateful. As the evening progressed, Dick had a lively conversation with our new friends. Often I saw him laughing with someone, and I smiled to myself, encouraged by his light-hearted appearance. *Maybe he's not as sick as we thought,* I mused, reaching for a feeble flicker of hope.

"How are you doing, Dick? Are those blood transfusions helping you?" asked one of the men.

"I'm doing fine, Jim," Dick answered with a grin. "I really think I'm getting better!"

Smiling, waving, and echoing our friends' "goodnight" farewells, we drove home—in silence. I watched Dick carefully as he turned the steering wheel and alternated from the accelerator to the brake. Pain lines were etched in his forehead, and he was gritting his teeth. *So, he played well to his audience. He always does.* This time his pleasant facade had fooled me too.

At home, Dick eased himself slowly through the front door, closed it quietly behind him, made his way painfully into our bedroom, then collapsed onto the bed. I helped him undress and wandered out to the living room to think.

Well, here you are Jeri. You're not married to the life of the party after all. You're living with a drained, sick, suffering man. There's not a thing in the world you can do to ease his misery. He isn't getting better, and he never will.

I lay on the couch with my head buried in my arms. I'd never felt so alone, and isolated by what seemed to me the inability of others to understand my heartache. In the eyes of our new friends and acquaintances, my emotional anguish surely must have appeared overdramatized. No one really knew what went on "backstage at the Krumroys" because we kept our suffering to ourselves. Dick was even better at hiding his feelings than I was.

My own actions weren't helping me either. While sympathizing with Dick—practically feeling his pain myself—I cried alone to hide my hurt from him. Dick seemed to sense my agony, and often tried to shield me from his pain. Both of us, by this unspoken pact to protect each other, were plunged into incredible loneliness.

There was also the matter of the damage the cancer was doing to his bones. They were becoming increasingly brittle. Sudden jerks or falls or even being jostled in a crowd could cause hairline fractures. Several weeks after the party, Dick broke a bone when he sneezed! He had to be hospitalized again, and this time I was faced with a grim new responsibility.

"Mrs. Krumroy," the nurse explained. "your husband's pain level is extremely high. The only relief we can give him now is through morphine. Before long he'll need injections around the clock every two or three hours. We want to teach you how to fill the hypodermic needles and administer the medication."

At first I practiced injecting water into oranges. Then I graduated to giving water shots to volunteer nurses. Finally the day came when I had to give Dick an injection at the hospital. The morphine had to be given slowly, and Dick's face was contorted with pain as the medication was injected into his body.

"You're doing fine, Mrs. Krumroy," the nurse encouraged me. "Morphine burns as it enters the bloodstream and, because it has to go in slowly, Mr. Krumroy will be quite uncomfortable until it begins to take effect."

I couldn't help hurting Dick, but I hated it. Why should I have to be the source of any more suffering for him? I wanted to help *ease* his pain, not inflict more!

The next morning dawned clear and warm. I stirred restlessly around the quiet house, getting myself ready for another work day. I felt uncertain, uneasy—I couldn't seem to climb out of my depression.

I dressed more carefully than usual. My bright red skirt and jacket complemented a new crimson and violet blouse perfectly.

"At least this will *look* cheerful," I mumbled, brushing my hair. I'd vowed never to let myself be seen in "sackcloth and ashes." There seemed no reason to inflict a drab, colorless mourner on my fellow workers. I wanted Dick to think I was handling things all right and to be proud of me.

Glancing in the mirror, I sighed, "I wish the puffiness around my eyes wasn't so obvious." I'd put ice cubes on them to reduce the swelling, but there had been too many tears last night. "A little makeup might help."

I was ready to go at last. Practicing, I smiled stiffly into the mirror. "It's a good thing these California people don't know me very well," I thought wryly. "My Ohio friends would be able to see what a mess I really am!"

I went out the back gate, across the little bridge and down the foot path that led to the Narramore Foundation's office building. As I hurried across the parking lot, a tall, blond man fell into step beside me.

"Good morning, Jeri. How's it going today?"

It was Jim Walker, one of the professional counselors who worked for the Foundation. "Oh, hi, Jim!" I flashed my newly-practiced smile at him. *Perhaps he won't notice my eyes. They feel so tired!*

"How's Dick doing? And how are you holding up?" Jim persisted.

"Oh, well, I guess you heard he's back at the City of Hope with another broken bone. But God is in control, and I'm doing just fine."

Speaking too quickly, my rambling words sounded strangely muddled even to my ears—too long an answer for such a simple question. I felt a flutter of fear when I glanced at Jim out of the corner of my eye. He was watching me intently. We walked in silence for a moment. His next words cut through my cheery, "spiritual" facade.

"Jeri," he chided gently, "why don't you forget your pride and get some help?"

Tears burned my eyes. I bit my lip and shook my head slightly. His question left unanswered, I rushed ahead of him toward the refuge of my upstairs office. All day I felt haunted by his question. "Get help . . . get help . . . get help . . . " The advice echoed in my mind as if God had spoken.

I rehearsed the events of the past few weeks in my thoughts. Several days before Dick went to the hospital, we sat together at a seminar. The speaker, Dr. Maurice Wagner, was introduced as an expert on depression. He was the senior counselor at The Narramore Foundation.

"As I've researched the Scriptures," Dr. Wagner said, "I've noticed that every place God deals with fear in the human mind, it is always associated with the feeling of aloneness. God says, 'Don't be afraid; I am with you.' Consider Psalm 34:4: 'I sought the Lord and he delivered me from all my fears.' The implication is that God delivers me by being with me.

"When the disciples were afraid their boat was going to sink, they woke Jesus up. He went up on deck and told the waves to be quiet, and then he said to his disciples, 'Don't you know that I'm here? There's nothing to be afraid of.'

"We can face anything in life as long as we know the Lord is with us. There's no problem in facing any situation because God can handle anything. Isaiah 41:10 is a classic verse, and it addresses the whole issue: "So do not fear, for I am with you; do not be dismayed, for I am your God. I will strengthen you and help you; I will uphold you with my righteous right hand (NIV).' "

Dr. Wagner's words drew me to him. He had just completed his first book and, following his talk, I hurried to the back of the auditorium to buy one. He smiled warmly as he autographed it for me.

After the lecture, I slowly made my way back to my office alone. My heart seemed ready to burst, and I fell to my knees and cried aloud, "God! I need help!"

Two days later, almost coincidentally, Dick and I had lunch with Dr. Wagner and his wife. We talked briefly about our personal lives, and I found myself inviting them to our home for dinner that night.

We had decided to have a barbeque on the patio. Dr. Wagner stepped outside with me for a moment as I checked the sizzling steaks.

"That's a gorgeous pool," he commented admiring the dancing sunlight on the water.

"I've been so depressed lately that I've felt like jumping into it and staying there!" I blurted. Realizing what I had said and to cover it up, I joked, "But I just had my hair done."

Dr. Wagner looked unruffled. "Well, I tell you what, Jeri. Why don't you come and see me instead?"

I had too much respect for God and for the Narramore Christian Foundation and too little courage to take my own life in the swimming pool. I knew there had to be a better way to deal with my pain and anger.

Jim's startling challenge had shaken my pride brutally. How could I face my friends after going to a counselor—a trained therapist no less? What would all those "healthy" Christians at work think of me if I needed psychological help after passing the tests and joining the staff? Wasn't my faith enough to see me through this ordeal?

In spite of increasing fears and endless excuses, I picked up the phone in my office and timidly made an appointment with Dr. Wagner. A friendly voice said that he would see me first thing the next morning!

His office was the last in a long row of similar counseling cubicles that faced each other across a quiet corridor. The door stood open, revealing a waiting room simply furnished with two or three chairs, a low table, a couple of tattered magazines, and a nondescript painting.

I glanced furtively down the hallway, and was relieved to find it empty. No one had seen me come. Choosing the chair that faced away from the door, I sat uncomfortably, hoping with all my heart that no one would recognize the back of my head!

What would talking to a professional counselor be like, I wondered nervously. It was impossible to imagine that in a few minutes I would be pouring out my pain to Dr. Wagner as if he were an old friend. He asked me about my relationship with Dick and seemed to understand the many complications that affected it.

"I feel so . . . alone . . . " Turning away from his searching gaze, I glanced helplessly at the floor. A sob escaped as my self-control vanished. "I feel so isolated and . . . " Again I couldn't go on. Dr. Wagner waited quietly as I wept, my face hidden in my hands.

"When we talk, I can't be honest. I can't tell Dick how awful I feel because I don't want him to feel guilty for being sick. His bones are so fragile he can't even hold me anymore, and now I have to give him his morphine!" Like raindrops splashing against a roof, my thoughts were scattered, my words unconnected. "I need love, too . . . I feel so lonely."

Alone. Pushed aside. Isolated. The agony of Dick's illness had carved a treacherous chasm between the two of us. "I've always been close to Dick, depended upon him, shared everything with him. Now I can't do that anymore."

"Do you understand what it is you're feeling, Jeri?" Dr. Wagner's tone challenged me to stop for a moment and think. "I feel . . . well, heartbroken, frustrated, terribly sad . . . I don't know."

"Is grief a good description of your feelings?"

"But Dick's still alive. Doesn't grief come *after* someone dies?"

"Jeri, by the time Dick dies, a large part of your grief will be over. You're grieving *now.*"

"I am? What do you mean?"

"Well, in simple terms, grief is the feeling of losing someone or something you love. Besides the sense of loss, there is an underlying hostility that says, 'I'm losing something and I resent it!'"

"So it's *grief* I'm feeling." I spoke softly, half to myself. "Grief . . . already? No wonder it hurts so much." I hadn't realized that for those who face a lingering death, grief begins before you say goodbye. Mine had begun the moment the doctor told me Dick had only two years to live.

"You know, Jeri, you've been a very dependent woman for a long time," Dr. Wagner explained. "Dependent people like you need a lot of tangible love. Everybody likes it, but you have an even greater need for it than, say, a more independent person."

"That means I'm weak, doesn't it?"

"Not at all!" Dr. Wagner's voice was emphatic. "What I'm saying is that you're continuously giving love to Dick— serving him, nursing him, waiting on him hand and foot— but he can't return that love to you in tangible ways because of his pain. So you feel starved for affection."

"Something else to commit to God, I suppose," I murmered.

"Not necessarily. We Christians believe that all our joy is to be found in the Lord. Yet God doesn't just reach out of heaven and pat us when we need it."

"*I need someone to help me!*" I began to cry again.

Would my tears never stop?

"Of course you do, Jeri. We all need each other. It's our mission to communicate God's love and joy to one another. But the people you've always shared with—your family and friends—are all in Ohio. Because you're not experiencing this communication, you're grieving."

I let his words speak to me. I wasn't just grieving about Dick's impending death; I was grieving over the loss of someone with whom to share my life and intimate thoughts.

"That's why I came to you, then—to be able to share," I said softly.

Dr. Wagner smiled at me. "Jeri, I'll stick by you the best I can."

Those words meant more to me at that moment than I could ever say. Here was a promise of support and help at the time of my life when I felt the most alone.

During those next months of agony, I leaned heavily on Dr. Wagner. He was the only person with whom I could openly share my feelings. By helping me to understand that grief begins before we say goodbye and that it is not forever, he set in motion a healing process that carried me through many emotional struggles. Guilt because of my conflicting feelings began to diminish as the awareness of my grief increased. At last I had some helpful insight in dealing with my emotions, not the least of which was *anger*.

4

Anger's Ashes

"Pass me that other vial, will you, Jeri?"

We were sitting at the table, preparing Dick's morphine. I'd stored the vials in the refrigerator so they would be ready when he needed them.

"Dick, Virginia suggested that you might try some needlepoint to help keep your mind off the pain," I volunteered.

"Needlepoint! That's for women—or sissies!"

"That's not so! Rosie Grier does needlepoint—a lot of athletes do."

"It's silly, Jeri. Whatever makes you come up with these ideas?"

I didn't answer him. He'd just have the last word anyway. I pulled my sweater around my shoulders and glanced at the clock.

"It's almost noon. Would you like some lunch?"

"Not hungry. You chilly? Winter will be here soon. I'd like you to go down to the hardware store and get a new furnace filter. It needs to be changed before we can start heating the house."

"But Dick, I don't know how. Who's going to change it?"

"It's easy. You can do it. After I'm gone you'll have to do it all the time."

A flash of heat washed over my face. *"After I'm gone... After I'm gone." How I hate those words!* Dick had fired them at me so often that I began to wonder if he were deliberately baiting me with them. I knew it was his way of dealing with his mortality—and helping me to face it. Yet the words cut and burned until I could hardly stand it. Anger quickly surfaced.

"First, pull the old filter out and find out what size it is. It's written right on the filter," Dick instructed. "Then go to the hardware store and pick up a new one. I'll tell you how to put it in when you get back."

Now furious, I drove to the shopping center. *This is Dick's job. Why do I have to do it?* At the store I glanced furtively around. *Just as I thought. Not another woman in sight. I've entered a man's territory.*

"May I help you?"

"I need to buy a new furnace filter," I squeaked, feeling foolish and totally out of place. Embarrassed and irritated, but with new filter in hand, I headed home.

"What did I do to deserve *this?*" I shouted at God. "I've got better things to do than to fix furnaces!"

In spite of my hostility, there was a certain sense of accomplishment when the task was completed. It wasn't all that difficult after all. I poured myself a cup of coffee, took it into the living room and sat down to enjoy it.

Now, Jeri, you really didn't have any trouble putting that filter in. You didn't even get dirty. Why were you so angry?

I began to realize that part of my reaction was from feeling threatened. I had a false concept of my role as wife and woman. In reality, the furnace needed a filter. Did it really make a difference who got it? It became my task because no one else was available. Taking care of the filter didn't destroy my femininity—only my perception of it!

I smiled as I recalled Dick's reaction to my suggestion of doing needlepoint. He, too, had assigned a sexual attribute to an asexual function. We both certainly had a lot of growing to do!

I was angry about the filter for another reason though. The weight of my responsibilities was becoming so heavy that any interruption in the day's routine added stress to what was already a pressure-cooker existence. We are usually frustrated when our normal schedules are disrupted, and it was happening all too frequently to me.

When extra chores or unexpected problems demanded time, I felt imposed upon. Accomplishment eluded me. If I weren't tracking down a furnace filter, I was doing our banking or picking up a prescription at the drug store. Run, run, run. My rear view mirror reflected a permanent frown.

As I discussed these feelings with Dr. Wagner, I began to see the reason why I had reacted so strongly to schedule changes. My father had never been flexible in dealing with change. When his routine was interrupted, he became angry and shouted at my mother. Although he never yelled at me, he was modeling the behavior that I later chose for myself.

As I recognized that my attitudes reflected my dad's behavior, Dr. Wagner helped me to understand that I do not have to be controlled by my dad's influence. Through the presence of the Holy Spirit, God has given me all I need to control my behavior.

Dr. Wagner suggested I make a conscious choice to transfer the authority for my behavior from my earthly father to my heavenly Counselor, who wants to help me through the changes. This thought has helped me to be much more flexible in situations that require change.

But this flexibility did not come overnight. Other problems stemmed from what seemed to be an endless process of giving up my own needs for Dick's. Before we moved to California, I sewed most of my clothes and made some of Dick's jackets. Sewing was the one thing about which I really felt competent, and Dick's enthusiasm for my ability gave me a sense of accomplishment. Then I had to give it up—there was just no time.

"Honey, I'd love a new dress," I sighed one Saturday morning. "I wish I could sit down and whip something together, but I don't know when I'd have the chance."

"Well, just go down and buy yourself something, and don't worry about it," he answered absently.

"Sometimes I really miss sewing." I stared wistfully into my steaming cup of coffee.

"Don't worry about it," Dick repeated, missing the point.

I didn't mind buying something ready-made, but deep inside I wanted to be creative. My clothing had a personal touch and was made more distinctive than the purchased pattern. I had been forced to relinquish still another part of myself.

My frustration was compounded when we moved a hospital bed into our living room. With lovely furniture in our home, both of us had enjoyed an orderly, uncluttered living area. I knew there was no better place for the offending bed because Dick was more comfortably located when visitors arrived and he could use it for rest during the day. There it sat, in the middle of all our activities, a constant, nagging reminder of our worsening ordeal.

The growing clutter added more confusion to our already unsettled circumstances. Everything in our lives seemed to be out of place. I was continually hostile and seemed powerless to do anything about it.

Combined with my fatigue and depression, the anger was sapping my strength. Once the initial heat of anger passed, resentment, bitterness, frustration, and depression surfaced. I felt hostile—and I hated myself for it.

God, I'm plagued by this anger. This trial is hopeless—it's never going to end. How can I make it through? I don't understand why I feel this way. Help me!

Finally I discussed my anger directly with Dr. Wagner.

"Is anger always sin?" I asked, feeling guilty.

"Of course not. Ephesians 4:26 says, 'Be angry, and yet do not sin.'" He smiled.

"What does that mean?"

"When Adam sinned, he became willful, self-determining. He no longer felt responsible to God. The root of most of our anger is this same self-will, or an anti-God feeling . . . ."

"Well, then it *is* sin," I countered. "Anything anti-God is sin, isn't it?"

"God only holds us accountable for reactions we can control, Jeri. Since anger springs from our unconscious link with Adam's sin, we can't control it. God holds us responsible for anger *after* it appears in our conscious minds. He looks to see what we *do* with it. That's the real key—how we *deal* with our anger."

During the next several weeks, I dug more deeply in my counseling sessions, into various aspects of anger. I learned that this feeling often begins with irritation, a reaction that wants to remove whatever interferes with our desires.

My anger and resentment wanted to eliminate Dick's cancer and our unpleasant circumstances. It was my rebellion against pain. When something unpleasant is imposed upon us, our freedom is threatened. If we can neither remove the threat nor escape, we react angrily.

My freedom to live a normal life with a healthy husband had been taken from me. Anger was a very real part of the grief I was feeling over that loss. Although I recognized the feeling as a normal part of the grief process, nevertheless I felt guilty, and even more depressed. I cried often.

I hid my tears from Dick in our bathrooms, laundry room, the garage—wherever I could run and weep without his knowledge. I remember one night in particular.

Looking sleeplessly out the window at a clear, midnight sky, I rested my chin on my arms. My tears turned the moon into a silvery blur. I stumbled into the bathroom and began to sob, "Lord, if you aren't going to take Dick home, please take me!" I wanted out. My ability to "love and to cherish in sickness" was rapidly dissolving.

Awakening to countless colorless mornings while Dick was in the hospital, I seemed always on my way to be with him. I would wake up limp, almost helpless under the blankets. The thought of crawling from the warmth and deciding what to wear, applying make-up, brushing my hair —it all seemed absurdly impossible. Weariness weighted down my arms and legs. My eyelids were heavy with sleep. How could I go on?

Part of my problem with depression stemmed from physical exhaustion. Instead of relaxing for an hour for lunch, I'd hurry home during my break to make Dick's lunch when he wasn't in the hospital. I'd inject him with morphine and scurry back to be a cheerful hostess at the Foundation.

"Why Dick? Why me?" I asked God those questions so many times that my whining must have sounded like a broken record. I thought that God had allowed this difficulty to come into our lives for a reason. But how could I honor God in the midst of such grim circumstances?

"Who are you angry at, Jeri?" Dr. Wagner asked one day.

"What do you mean?" I avoided his eyes.

"*Who* are you angry at? You're expressing anger, but you haven't told me who it is you're angry at."

"I'm not angry at anyone!"

The question spun around in my mind for days. Suddenly the answer struck me.

"I'm mad at God!" I blurted the next time we talked.

"That's right. It was God who set this thing up in the first place. You've finally found the author of your situation. You know God could make Dick well, and . . ."

"I have a *right* to be angry!" I spat out the words before he could go on.

"Sure you do. And you're wise to admit it. Some people believe that because they couldn't be angry at their parents without punishment, they dare not be angry at God. They fear that they would be destroyed, so they deny their anger.

"We get upset at our children," Dr. Wagner continued, "when we don't understand how they feel. We're offended. 'Don't you *ever* say you hate me,' we yell. But God understands our feelings and is not threatened by them.

"One of the great messages of the book of Jonah is the prophet's anger at God. All God said was, 'Do you have good reason to be angry?' (Jonah 4:4). God wasn't upset."

Even so, it was several weeks before I could express my anger at God openly. The night that I finally vented it openly remains vivid in my memory. Dick had been suffering without relief for two years. My irritation and aloneness had reached a scorching climax. Sick of my continuous turmoil, I stood in my backyard, looked up at the stars, and spoke icily.

"I can't feel you, God, but I know you're there. I think you're pretty rotten to let this thing go on and on and *on*. I can't see any sense to it. I don't know what you expect from me," I raged, half-expecting God to strike me dead.

"I don't know how you ever expect me to praise you and give you thanks for what Dick and I've been going through. You're certainly not doing anything to deserve it. Your Word says we grow through trials, but why do you have to take it out on Dick so *I* can learn? He won't even be here to see the results!"

For a few moments I said nothing more. Intellectually I knew God loved me, but my heart was aching too much to feel it. Slowly, I began to bargain with God! Not once in my life had I ever made a promise to the Lord saying, "If you'll do *this,* I'll do *that."* Yet, there under the silent stars I found myself praying, "I don't want my anger, Lord. You can have it. If you'll give me back the peace and joy of my salvation, I'll share my experiences with others."

I stood quietly as a soft wind blew. From somewhere deep within, a sense of God's presence began to swell. "I love you, Jeri. I paid a price for you." Those words burned indelibly upon me and spoke to my heart. This was a turning point for me, a moment when anger began to give way to love. I didn't realize until much later that anger and resentment are emotions that were separating me from feeling God's closeness. Once I acknowledged my feelings and relinquished them to God, I was able to sense God's presence in my life again.

During the following weeks, two events convinced me that God had acted upon my plea. The first occurred while I was visiting Dick in the hospital. "Jeri, there's been a change in you lately," he observed.

"What do you mean?"

"It's your attitude. Somehow it's more positive. You don't seem to be as upset as you've been the past year or so."

I cringed a little, realizing that my feelings had not been as carefully hidden as I had supposed. Nevertheless, I was happy because this reflected the work that God was doing in my life. I was learning to accept without hostility those things that I could not change.

This lesson could be learned only through the hardship of my trial. I was beginning to feel more compassion for Dick's suffering and thinking less of my own inconvenience and situation. This ordeal wasn't pleasant for him, either.

A humbling thought came to me after Dick's remark about my change of attitude. I hadn't really made a bargain with God at all! He had made one with me. As long as I was miserable, angry, and locked into irritation and resentment, I was useless to God and of no comfort to Dick. My constant desire was to serve the Lord but, before I could be of any service, I had to relinquish not only my anger, but also my husband, to God.

Part of my release came from understanding that anger of itself is not sinful. If I sinned, it was in my desire for vengeance. Vengeance implies ownership. I had decided that Dick belonged to me, and sin entered the picture when I harbored my anger against God for taking him away. I had fought God at every turn, and I'd only ended up resenting Dick as well.

The counseling sessions helped me to know I didn't have to be sorry for my anger. That would only create unnecessary guilt. If I needed forgiveness, it was for my lack of love and for the way I handled my anger—not for feeling it.

Unfortunately, my backyard "bargain" and new sense of commitment didn't mark the end of the struggle. Often during the next months, I would carry my anger to Dr. Wagner. I was in the laboratory on the one side and in the instruction chamber on the other. Battles between Jeri Krumroy and anger continued to flare, but I always wanted God's will and made up my mind to keep trying, even though it meant a struggle between self-will and the will of God.

Painfully, I've come to realize that a commitment to God is not necessarily an overnight, once-and-for-all cure to our problems. Anger can be triggered by memories, by faces, by familiar surroundings. Even after we think we're free, ugly feelings can resurface when least expected.

Does this mean we should give up in despair? No. The Apostle Paul felt the same frustration. "The good that I wish, I do not do," he wrote. "But I practice the very evil that I do not wish . . . wretched man that I am! Who will set me free from the body of this death?" (Romans 7:19, 24).

Paul's answer gives us all hope. "Thanks be to God through Jesus Christ our Lord . . . ! There is therefore now no *condemnation* for those who are in Christ Jesus" (Romans 7:25–8:1).

God understands our frailty, and forgiveness is always extended to us. Our task is to recommit our lives each time we fail. Eventually, as we grow in Christ, our strength to overcome sin will increase, and we hope to live victoriously after death.

The second event that affirmed my bargain with God was an invitation to speak to a group of women at a luncheon. I was to talk about facing grief. At first I shied away from the task; it seemed too painful. Yet I was reminded of my new covenant and, reluctantly, I agreed. That day a woman committed her life to Christ after listening to me speak. I prayed with her after the meeting.

Driving home I felt much love and gratitude to God. *How much is a soul worth?* I wondered. The suffering I had experienced was small compared to what Christ had done for me.

Thousands of years ago the prophet Isaiah wrote some extraordinary words which Jesus later used in his ministry.

> The Spirit of the Lord God is upon me; because the Lord hath anointed me to preach good tidings unto the meek; he hath sent me to bind up the broken-hearted, to proclaim liberty to the captives, and the opening of the prison to them that are bound . . . to comfort all that mourn . . . to give unto them beauty for ashes, the oil of joy for mourning, the garment of

praise for the spirit of heaviness . . . that he might be glorified.

Isaiah 61:1–3 (KJV)

God wants the ashes of our burned-out anger and the cold embers of our useless hostility in exchange for opportunities to serve. I was beginning to discover the delight in discarding those worthless remains, the joy of becoming a messenger to the sorrowing, the hurting, the mourning. Beauty for ashes—a bargain indeed!

5

"I Need to Go On!"

The glittering Pacific ocean played hide-and-seek with us as Dick and I followed the winding road toward the picturesque little village of San Simeon, California. We wanted to make the most of the time we had left together, so we decided to do some of the things we'd always wanted to do. Outings such as this had done wonders for us both.

Dick and I were discovering the value of living one day at a time. The gentle past, the horror-filled future—neither is a good place for the mind to dwell. Knowing that God is in control *today* is the underlying peace that passes understanding. We had decided to have some fun together before we had to say goodbye.

The family photo albums we put together after our move to California contain an array of scenes and a variety of settings, with Dick and me smiling cheerfully in every snapshot. We went to Disneyland, Knott's Berry Farm, Universal Studios. As the dates beneath the photographs moved relentlessly ahead, Dick's face grew thinner, his hair more sparse and grey.

No matter where we went or what we did, we could not forget our sadness. Unfortunately, escape from grief would be impossible before Dick's eventual death. I knew that even then a final period of mourning would undoubtedly occur.

Nevertheless, Jesus taught that "each day has enough trouble of its own" (Matthew 6:34). We had determined not to borrow tomorrow's tears. By living one day at a time, Dick and I *could* prepare ourselves for the uncertainties of life and the certainty of death.

One way we had decided to prepare was to build memories, and this time Dick had chosen to visit Hearst Castle at San Simeon, up the California coast. He was intrigued by its structure and the engineering that had gone into it. The builder in him was as alive as ever.

Although hairpin curves caused him to brace himself painfully time and again, Dick seemed to enjoy himself as we made our way toward the famous landmark. Before long, the rolling fields parted, and we saw twin Spanish-style towers crowning the highest hill. A late morning sun set the castle aglow like a white jewel against green velvet. Beyond the hill, the sapphire-blue ocean glimmered in the sunlight.

Followed by our friends, Jim and Libbie, who had come in their own car, we drove up the entry lane and parked. Since Dick had purchased our tickets in advance, we began to look for the starting point of our tour. Then I noticed a large sign.

**Over 300 steps to climb.
Persons who experience difficulty
climbing or descending steps are
advised not to attempt tours.**

My heart sank.

"Dick, did you see that sign?"

"Yes, I saw it. But I've bought the tickets, and I'm going," he snapped.

Tour Three would give him the best perspective of the famous building's construction. I felt protective, but I didn't want to ruin our little vacation.

We joined Jim and Libbie and followed the well-informed young man leading our group. The more steps we climbed, the more pain registered on Dick's face. He laughed and chatted with our friends, never mentioning his discomfort. But pain had tinted his complexion a greyish hue, and the tell-tale lines of agony made deeper furrows in his forehead.

"Dick," I whispered, "let me find an elevator down."

"No," he hissed through clenched teeth, "I'm fine."

By the time we reached the third floor, I knew he couldn't make it back. Spotting a guard, I walked over to him.

"Excuse me. My husband is ill. Is there an elevator we can use?"

"Right over there, Ma'am," he pointed.

Turning to Jim and Libbie, I announced, "We're going down in the elevator."

"Okay, Jeri. We'll meet you later." Libbie nodded knowingly.

In the elevator Dick fumed in silence. How he hated to have a woman tell him what to do. How I hated to be the one to do it.

"You'll be glad later, honey," I comforted, forcing a smile. "Jim and Libbie understand. It's only been a couple of years since their son died of leukemia."

We stayed overnight in a nearby motel; our friends were in adjoining rooms. Dick spent a fitful night, and his injections did little to ease his worsening pain. I made a mental note to ask the doctor to increase his dosage when we got back home.

In the morning Dick put on his best smile to greet our friends for breakfast, unwilling to admit or give in to his suffering. I was grateful to know that Jim and Libbie understood how we were feeling in this "let's pretend" game.

Dick happily waved good bye to them as they headed northward for the rest of their vacation, then gently took my hand.

"I love you, Jeri."

"I love you, sweetheart," I responded. In all the years we'd been married, Dick had never let a day go by without telling me that. He leaned down and kissed me on the cheek. Silently, we turned and strolled hand in hand to our car. It would be a long drive home, but Dick chose a road with fewer curves.

We stopped in Oxnard for lunch. Pain had taken Dick's appetite, but he sipped a malt while we sat together, chatting.

"Jeri, I don't want you to go back to see Dr. Wagner anymore," he said matter-of-factly.

"What?" I was stunned. Dick had not been overly supportive when I sought professional help, but these words were a surprise. "But Dick—why not?"

"You're doing okay now. He's helped you, and you're fine."

Do you think counseling is like going to the doctor for some kind of magic pill to make everything all right? I need to talk out my feelings with a trustworthy friend. We had no long time and trusted friends in California in whom to confide. Dr. Wagner had skillfully been helping me to probe—to uncover my feelings, to identify them, to deal with them. He'd listened to my complaints without judging me, and he had become my friend.

Perhaps this process of sharing openly with each other is what the Apostle James had in mind when he wrote, "confess your faults to one another, and pray for one another, that ye may be healed" (James 5:26 KJV).

I was not yet healed. I was the one who had to go on and face life alone. I wasn't ready; I needed more help.

"No, Dick," I refused. "I need to go on."

He looked dejected. "I thought I could be the one to help you."

What could I say? It would be cruel to dump on him all of the conflicting emotions I was feeling as a result of his illness. He had his own grief to work through, too. I realized that Dick felt rejected, and perhaps even a little jealous that I was relying on another man.

Understanding how he felt, I was determined to make clear to him that I still loved him. Somehow I'd have to show him that my new insights into myself and our problem were going to make me a better person, capable of going on.

Back in the car, we drove in silence. I knew that my two refusals to go along with Dick's wishes had shocked him. In reality, I was a little surprised by my determination to be more assertive. I'd never refused his wishes before, but this time I was right. I could not let him intimidate me into backing down.

Near Los Angeles I finally asked, "How do you feel, Dick?"

"I'm fine. I'm all right." He forced his words between clenched teeth. Dick was anything but all right.

I took him back to the hospital the next morning. He had suffered another fracture. It hardly seemed worth it at the time, but I knew that years from now the fading snapshots would make me grateful that we took the time to enjoy these trips.

Yet the pleasure of the outing at Hearst Castle was marred as much by my conflict with Dick as by his new fracture. Submission to Dick had been the most effortless thing in the world for me. One of the few things I thought that I understood in the Bible when we were married was that a wife should be in subjection to her husband. That being the case, I had been doing everything just right. Dick *always* had his way.

His strong, persuasive attitude had given him success in business. He'd had to make quick decisions, and in most cases, they were right. People admired Dick's confidence, his courage, his strength. He was widely respected as a man of integrity and fortitude.

All of this made me feel secure, loved, and delightfuly comfortable. I respected his opinion much more than my own. The truth was, Dick *did* have good ideas. Whenever he asked me what I thought about something, I wondered why he even bothered. I appreciated his interest, but my low self-esteem made my opinions seem irrelevant.

I was unaware of the negative aspects in our constrasting personalities until the day Dick suffered his cerebral hemorrhage. Then, all at once, the horrifying reality struck me: I might actually have to face life alone! Instead of preparing myself, I was overwhelmed with relief when Dick was able to handle matters again. I tuned him out when he tried to explain our finances to me, and remained woefully dependent on him.

Now the dreaded responsibility of facing life alone

loomed high above me like a cresting tidal wave. The inevitable was certain. The sands of time had begun to build a tiny mountain at the bottom of the hour-glass. I could no longer live in denial. I would have to make it some way—even if it meant having conflict with Dick. I shared my frustration in continued counseling with Dr. Wagner.

"Just learning to handle every day tasks seems insurmountable! It's not just learning how to check the water and the oil in the car—or remembering to pay the utilities. It's balancing the checkbook and figuring out taxes. Even if I hire an accountant, I'm going to have to know *something* about managing my money!

"Dick wants to have me become acquainted with an attorney—but I feel smothered by all of the information he keeps feeding me. Every new instruction seems like a higher mountain to scale than the last one! He's always handled all of our business before—I can't follow any of it!"

Together Dr. Wagner and I began to unravel the tangled yarn of my dependency by tracing the threads back to my early years at home with mom and dad.

"Jeri, from childhood, your parents didn't see you as an independent person. They maintained your dependence upon them by making your decisions for you, by telling you what you had to do. Isn't that true?"

"Yes. I didn't have a lot of choice in many situations."

"This extended beyond your early years into your teenage years," Dr. Wagner continued, "you were still dependent upon your folks long after you should have been developing a sense of autonomy."

"I know one thing—I sure would have been lost without them before I married Dick. They were a big part of my world."

"That's right. Then when Dick came along, he began to replace your mother. The new formula was Dick plus Jeri equals a whole person."

"When we became Christians, God was part of the formula, too," I objected.

"Yes. *God* plus Dick plus Jeri would equal a whole Jeri.

In a sense that's right. In a normal marriage, the companion-ship and interdependency create that kind of interaction — a person feels more complete with his mate. Your situation went beyond that."

"But that's the way I thought it should be . . . " I felt saddened by this insight, yet I could see the truth in what he was telling me. Being interdependent also meant the risk of being my own unique self.

"Another thing, Jeri, the pattern for marriage you saw in your home didn't provide you with a clear example of how a marital relationship is meant to function."

This was true, too. My parents were good people. They took my two sisters and me to church every Sunday. Although they weren't active Christians at the time, they kept drinking and smoking out of our home. Dad made a good living which was intensely important to him. Thriftily managing the family's money, he had put mother on an allowance.

Dad must have been more generous than he intended, because I can still remember mother pulling me aside one day and whispering furtively, "Jeri, if the house ever catches fire, I want you to promise to do something for me."

I must have looked at her blankly. Why would the house catch on fire?

She hurried on with her instructions, "I want you to go into my bedroom and pull out the second drawer. Jeri, I've got a hundred dollars hidden under there. *But whatever you do, don't tell your father!*"

Although mother always seemed fearfully to be work-ing her way around dad, the fact was, she had the more dominant personality. Dad was a passive man, yet had a quick, hot temper. If mother felt faint after a hurried trip to town, she didn't want to upset father. He was angry when-ever she was ill, in fact he exploded whenever one of us children was sick.

Dad guarded our finances and, if mother had managed to put away a little extra money from her allowance, she didn't want him to think that he was giving her too much. "Don't tell your father!" was the command that told us mother was wrapping dad around her little finger as usual, but it was his quick, hot temper that she sought to escape. She learned how to manipulate him to get her own way.

Sometimes when dad was angry, he'd yell at mom in a rage, then give her the silent treatment. Finally, mom would send me over to the neighbors — without dad's knowledge — to invite them over so that he would be forced to break his silence.

Other times mom put her friend, Faye, up to talking my dad into buying something mom wanted. "Come on, stingy," Faye said, "don't be such a tightwad." Faye would say what mom was thinking, and dad would give in.

Unavoidably, the contrast in their personalities led to bickering. I remember lying one night on my second-story bedroom floor, listening to them argue. Back and forth, back and forth, the conversation went, voices rising and falling with emotion.

Never, I told myself that night, *never will there be fighting in my home when I get married.* I was determined to have a different kind of marriage.

"Jeri, in a sense you've been refusing to handle conflict or confront problems. Instead, you've left the responsibility up to Dick."

"Isn't that submission?" I objected. "Lots of marriages are structured like ours."

"No, Jeri, it's compliance. Submission is different. It *chooses* to be subordinate. The person chooses to give in. It isn't because of a fear of conflict. A truly submissive wife has herself pretty well figured out. She knows what she wants, and what she really wants is to be pleasing, so she submits."

"I want to please Dick!"

"Of course you do. When you married him you'd had little experience in making up your own mind. It was almost impossible for you to know how to say, 'This is what I really want.' You hadn't defined yourself clearly. What was your inclination when faced with a decision?"

"To go along with whatever Dick offered."

"And if it turned out wrong?"

"I'd resent it, but . . ."

"But you never said anything."

"Right."

"That's *compliance,* not submission."

I was beginning to understand. In a sense, my idea of submission had been like the little boy who kept standing up in the car. Finally his mother told him to sit down before she paddled him.

"Are you sitting down?" she asked.

"I'm sitting down on the outside," he replied, "but on the inside, I'm standing up!"

God sees the *inside,* and the Word of God says we should be "transformed by the renewing of your mind, that you may prove what the will of God is, that which is good and acceptable and perfect" (Romans 12:2).

It is only when the inner and the outer *agree* that we can have peace. Anything else—including compliance—is hypocrisy.

How I wished I'd understood all this earlier in our marriage! I discovered something wonderful in it, too. When the Bible says, "Submit yourselves to one another," it speaks to men as well as to women, wives as well as husbands in the church family. We can all choose to subordinate ourselves to one another. Anyone who demands submission receives only servitude. By contrast, when submission is given willingly by both partners, the sharing can become beautiful.

This understanding gave me strength as Dick weakened and began to slip away. Necessity forced me to take more initiative in our lives, to tackle problems whether I felt capable or not. Through tough, painful growth, I was reevaluating myself, learning to believe that I was able, with God's help, to face the difficult days ahead.

6

Practically Prepared

"How's it going, Grandpa?"

"Just great! Here—let me show you this picture of little Karin. Isn't she a beauty? Healthy, too!" Dick pulled out his "brag book" and showed our friend and neighbor, Tom, the latest pictures of our granddaughter.

"She's a pretty little thing, all right."

"And guess what? Bob and Lonnie called last night. They're expecting, too! Bob was so tickled! Tom, can anyone be better blessed than to receive two grandbabies in one year?"

"That is good news, Dick! I really enjoyed meeting Bob and Lonnie when they were here for Christmas. Say—what's this?" Tom pointed to some needlepoint at the foot of Dick's bed.

Dick grinned at me sheepishly. "Looks crazy, doesn't it? You know Jack at the Foundation? He's been doing some needlepoint, and he convinced me to try it. Jeri suggested it a while ago, but—anyway, I'm going to make one for each of my grandchildren. They'll have something from their Grandpa Krumroy."

"A lot of guys are doing needlepoint, I guess," Tom offered.

"Yeah. I met a retired plumber at the craft store the day Jeri took me to get this. He was getting supplies for a new project—looked pretty tough to me. It keeps my mind off the—it keeps me busy."

As I walked Tom to the door, he nodded toward the back yard. "I'll come by later in the week and pull those weeds for you, Jeri. The winter rains really encouraged them to grow."

"Oh, Tom, thank you! My arm's been giving me trouble, and with all the other things I have to do . . . "

"Don't worry about it, Jeri. I'm glad to help."

I was grateful for friends who saw places where they could help and made themselves available. It had always been hard for both of us to ask for help, and I somehow never found myself able to call on those who would offer, "If there's anything I can do, don't hesitate . . . "

Yet when someone rang the doorbell with a casserole in hand, or telephoned to say, "I'm on the way to the drug store; can I get you anything?" I delighted in their thoughtfulness. Specific offers for specific kinds of help never injured our pride, and spared me the necessity of trying to decide what I really needed at the moment. More than once I wept with gratitude at the tender concern showed by Tom and other new friends for Dick and me.

Several days later Tom came over early to take care of the yardwork.

"What's he doing out there?" Dick demanded.

"He's helping me get the flower bed cleaned out. I don't know how I could have done it without him; my arm's been so sore lately."

Silence followed as Dick soberly stared at the spring-time sunlight dancing crazily across the water in the pool. He sighed and turned to me.

"I'm jealous," he muttered suddenly.

"You're *what?*" It was so unusual for Dick to express himself this way that I thought for a moment I had misunderstood.

"I'm jealous," he repeated. "I wish I could be the one out there helping you."

"I wish you could, too, honey. But you help me in ways that are far more important than weed-pulling!" At that moment a warm flood of appreciation filled me, and I thought my heart would burst. "I love you so much, Dick. I don't think I can manage without you!"

Dick's eyes brimmed with tears. "I don't want to leave you, Jeri."

"I know," I whispered. "I know. But Dick, if I had to endure the pain you suffer, I'd want to die." My voice cracked, and it hurt my throat to swallow.

"I don't want to die, Jeri." He wiped his eyes and picked

up his needlepoint.

I went into the bathroom and ran the shower full blast to cover the sound of my sobbing. How I wished the crying would stop. Dick had been sick for more than two and a half years now, and there was never a day without tears anymore.

I knew Dick had no fear of death, and that he welcomed the knowledge that he would be with Jesus. I sensed that he was really saying, "I don't think you can make it on your own, and I want to stay around to take care of you and protect you."

All these years could have been so different! Why haven't we ever come to the point where we can communicate openly — we should have started doing that a long time ago. I don't know if I'll ever be able to reach you the way I'd like to.

Later that week I talked to Dr. Wagner about my excessive crying.

"All of these tears are unhealthy!" I wept.

"Not at all, Jeri," he countered. "Tears indicate an overload to the mind. They don't indicate weakness — just an overload of feelings."

"Crying is never unhealthy, then?"

"Well, if it went on ceaselessly — kind of a superficial spirituality or professional mourning — one would need to examine the reasons for tears. When a person is faced with one emotional trauma after another, tears help balance the load. Crying can help you release your tensions so you can reason things out."

"Dick says he never cried in front of anybody until after he accepted Christ, but he shed lots of tears afterwards," I reflected. "It's sad not to be able to cry at all. I only wish I could control it better."

"What do you think crying does *for* you, Jeri?"

"Well, if it indicates an overload, it must be some kind of safety device — sort of a washing and sorting of our deepest feelings. Maybe it's just a way of releasing grief, instead of hoarding it. I must have the cleanest eye balls in the world!"

A few days later I took Dick back to the hospital. He was

feeling more pain—this time in his shoulder. After taking X-rays and examining them meticulously, Dick's doctor shook his head and sighed slowly.

"Another hairline fracture, Dick. Too much driving and walking. Breaks can occur almost spontaneously, now. Any jolt or bump will almost certainly cause a fracture. I want you to use your wheel chair more often, Dick, and I don't want you behind a steering wheel anymore. Jeri will have to sit in the driver's seat from now on."

The doctor let his words sink in. It was impractical for Dick to lie idle in his bed; he was far more comfortable moving around. We continuously tried to protect him from bumps and falls, while allowing him freedom. Now another measure of Dick's independence was gone—and a new responsibility was added to my list.

"While you're here, Dick" the doctor spoke quietly, "I'd like to give you a little more radiation therapy."

Driving home alone, I felt tense with irritation. "How *long* will this go on, God?" It seemed we were caught in a web, suspended in eternity, with no escape.

While Dick was receiving radiation therapy two days later, the doctor expressed his own frustration. "Well, Dick, that's it. We've done about all we can do with this."

"Wh—what do you mean?" Dick stammered.

"I just mean that radiation won't help you any more."

Dick fumed as we talked about the incident later. "What a terrible thing to say! Why did he have to tell me that?"

Facing the stark reality of death is difficult for anyone. Dick and I were becoming experts on grief. We'd learned that grief comes in stages—denial, bargaining, anger, depression and, finally, acceptance. We bounced in and out of denial. We'd say, "No, this can't be happening to us," or Dick would insist, "I really think I'm getting better."

As Christians, we faced a further complication. Would God heal? In our case, neither Dick nor I felt that healing would occur. I had prayed half-heartedly toward that end when we first learned about Dick's illness. I did not sense a God-given faith in Dick's healing nor were we encouraged to pray toward divine healing. We did pray, often, for release from pain. While each Christian has a different experience, and we knew many had been delivered by God's healing touch, the Lord seemed to have a different plan for our lives.

Nonetheless, it hurt to be confronted by the doctors each time Dick slipped further downhill, although we thought it would be cruel to be kept in ignorance about Dick's condition. Sometimes it is a great sin against a dying person not to tell that person the truth. Honesty is important at all levels of communication. A terminally ill person gains no security from fairy tales and euphemisms. Honesty, tempered with compassion and sensitivity, enables the dying to prepare.

Jesus set a beautiful example as he agonized on the cross. The Lord looked lovingly down to John and said, "Behold, your mother. Mother, behold your son." Jesus had opportunity to care for his family before he died.

Dick needed that opportunity, too. That didn't make it easy; we walked a tight wire above a chasm of despair. Knowing what was happening was a hellish thing even though not knowing would have been so much worse.

Oddly, while Dick struggled with the physical realities of his illness, he seemed to have no trouble in dealing with the practical aspects of preparing for his death. We updated our wills, and we planned his funeral together so that I would not be faced with that necessity after he died.

"You can have a memorial service here, Jeri, but I want to be buried in Ohio. You can have the funeral in our church there. The mortuary in Ohio will work out the details with the mortuary here, so you shouldn't have to make too many phone calls when the time comes."

I nodded numbly. It was important, I knew, to get these details settled. Yet it seemed ghoulish, too. I was glad Tom had volunteered to go along with me to make the arrangements.

At the mortuary I filled out the necessary forms. I had to know Dick's Social Security number and his mother's maiden name. I signed release forms and filled out a financial statement. As Dick had requested, I phoned the mortuary in Ohio, and the two businesses worked together on arranging for Dick's body to be flown back East. The funeral director reminded me to sign a release form at the City of Hope, permitting the hospital to notify the mortuary and to release Dick's body to them when the time came.

Then it was time to select the casket. My legs went limp as I entered the showroom. There was a surprising variety, and for a minute I thought, *This is like looking at a dress on a rack and trying to imagine how it will fit without trying it on.*

Imagining how Dick would look in a casket tied my stomach in knots. I could see his gray head placed softly on a small powder blue pillow. I wished this decision were over. I finally selected a rich-looking wood casket because Dick, having been a builder, loved the warm tones of wood.

I called the church in Ohio and asked the pastor to help with arrangements there. Dick made sure I covered every detail. We made a list of the agencies we would have to notify such as banks, insurance companies, Social Security, and gave it to our attorney so he could handle that process for me.

It was hard for Dick and me to talk about all of this, but I was grateful that we did. It gave Dick a great sense of assurance that he had cared for me, provided for me, and protected me as much as possible, and it set the stage for the day when he would be able to release his sense of responsibility for me. In a way, he faced as much a struggle in relinquishing me to God as I did in giving him up.

"Jeri," he suggested one day, "let's go for a ride. I want to buy you a new car."

"A car? Why?"

This one is going to need to be replaced in a year or two. At first I thought you could take a man along with you to buy it, because salesmen sometimes take advantage of widows. But I think I'd rather help you myself."

I was thankful that Dick was planning that far ahead for me—the thought of making any major purchase alone terrified me.

As we walked around the car lot, Dick leaned heavily on his cane. His face reflected the agony of every step. *I wish you had let me bring the wheel chair, honey.* I was tempted to suggest that we return another day, except that we couldn't be certain of any better days.

"This is my going away present to you, sweetheart," he said tenderly.

These words were a stab right to my heart. I bit the inside of my lip and squeezed his arm. My throat felt tight and it hurt to swallow, but I'll cherish the closeness of that moment forever.

"Dick," I finally said, "thank you for doing this for me. I want a car that will have plenty of room and be comfortable for you."

We selected a two-door car with separate seats in the front that could move six ways with plenty of room at the side. I could move my seat close to the steering wheel, and Dick could stretch out his legs and relax. The only problem we could see was that the doors didn't lock automatically.

"You'll have to lock both doors manually." Dick sounded doubtful, and I began to feel uneasy. *What if I forget. What if I leave a door unlocked? Dick always locks the doors, and*—"Wait a minute," I blurted, "I'm a big girl. Surely I can remember to lock two car doors."

Dick eyed me with amusement. "Of course you can," he declared. How I needed that affirmation!

The car would not be delivered for six weeks and, as the days went by, Dick began to clean out filing cabinets and desk drawers. He introduced me to our lawyer and our accountant.

"You'll be more comfortable with them after I'm gone if you get to know them now," he explained.

I died inside—again. *You tell the doctors you feel better, and you play a good game of pretend with our friends. But for me, it's always, "After I'm gone."* I stared absently out the kitchen window. I *did* appreciate all of Dick's efforts to prepare me for the time when he would no longer be beside me, but I hated to be reminded of why it was necessary. The trouble is, my dear, dear husband—the heart can never be prepared completely.

7

Demolished on Impact

"Salt?"

"No thanks."

The sounds of silverware scraping and ringing against china filled our little dining room.

"Ketchup please . . . thanks."

We sat mutely at the supper table. Staring blankly at my waterglass, I couldn't think of another thing to say to Dick. We'd already talked about the weather, the letter from our daughter that had arrived that afternoon, and the football game that had delayed dinner by twenty minutes.

I glanced outside. A gentle breeze played with the poolside garden, tossing the flowers around softly. *So little time,* I mused. *Yet we never seem to talk anymore.* I was trying to get up the courage to verbalize this thought, when Dick braced himself with the table and rose slowly to his feet. The furrows in his forehead told me it wouldn't be long before he would need another shot of morphine. Fumbling for his cane, he turned carefully toward the bedroom. Soon I heard the all-too-familiar voice of the play-by-play announcer putting all the enthusiasm he could muster into another four quarters.

I jerked the dirty dishes off the table and set them clattering on the sink. *You're not going to ignore me, Dick Krumroy. Game or no game! No television is going to take my place—if I can help it!* A scheme began to form in my mind. Soon a sly smile loosened my tightly closed lips. *Why didn't I think of this before?*

My plan went into action well into the third quarter. Standing brazenly in front of the television set, I started to unbutton my blouse. Dick leaned impatiently to see around me. I blocked his view even more.

"A pretty girl is like a melody . . . " I sang suggestively. Waving my blouse in front of him I did a pirouette and then let the blouse drop to the floor.

Item by item I disrobed, my voice partially drowning the "third and goal to go" announcements coming from the set behind me.

"What on earth are you doing, Jeri?"

I kept singing and wiggling provocatively.

"What are you doing?" he repeated. "I can't see the television!"

"What does it look like I'm doing?" I sang.

"It looks very much like you are taking your clothes off and blocking out the game!"

"That's right!" Dick's bewildered expression amused me, and I giggled. "I just wanted to see if I have any of my old charm left." I grinned at him, winked, and finished my "routine" with an exaggerated wiggle.

Dick looked at me from head to toe, smiled sagely, and clicked off the remote control. "C'mon over here, sweetie. You're still my sweetheart—always will be." His bad imitation of Humphrey Bogart made us both laugh.

"Jeri, you're still as pretty as the day I met you. You were so delicate, standing there in your stocking feet! You'll never lose your charm." Dick caressed my cheek, then gently rubbed the back of my neck.

"It's kind of hard to compete with the television," I chided gently.

"I'm sorry, sweetheart. It's not you I'm trying to escape. The games are distracting, and they help me keep my mind off the pain."

"I know. I'm just feeling a little resentful," I confessed.

Dick leaned over and kissed me tenderly. I laughed, and soon we were chattering and chuckling as we'd done in years gone by. We'd recovered the glow of our romance, and I began to feel complete. Later I made hot cocoa with marshmallows, and we sat together enjoying the silence. It was the most refreshing evening we'd spent in months.

It didn't matter which team scored the most points in football that night. I had won the greatest victory, for I'd been able to communicate with Dick effectively.

It doesn't take grief to cause problems in communication. They are common in every friendship, family, and marriage. Most of these problems, I was beginning to discover, were caused by what Dr. Wagner had termed "three men in a tub" — hostility, guilt, and fear.

Hostility says, "I don't like you." The other person swiftly picks up the message and feels that he doesn't belong.

Guilt says, "I don't like me, so you won't either!" Again, separation occurs. This guilty feeling may not even have a foundation in truth.

Fear is another lonely feeling. It says, "I'm afraid of you," or "I'm afraid of me." If a person is fearful, he will not allow friendship to grow. The threat of rejection and hurt is too powerful. In matters of love, the sense of incompetence is overwhelming.

With Dr. Wagner's help, I was able to recall an incident in my childhood which had added to my inadequate self-image. Through the usual family "system of justice," I had been unfairly accused of wrong doing. I knew I was innocent but, when mother suggested that I apologize to dad, I nodded mutely.

My seven-year-old body trembled as I slowly mounted the staircase to his attic bedroom. What would he do to me? What would he say? Hesitantly, I tapped on the door, then slowly turned the knob.

"Daddy . . . " I whispered, " . . . I'm sorry . . . " My voice broke under the load of self-imposed guilt. Dad put his arms around me, and I crawled into bed with him. When I looked up at his face, through my tears, I saw that he was crying, too.

In a sense I had let my poor self-image affect my relationship with Dick. Because I assumed I wasn't good enough for him, I seldom let him know my real feelings, especially if we disagreed. Throughout our marriage, Dick and I had serious problems in communicating. My experiences with such house rules as "don't tell your father" left me unskilled in expressing myself honestly. I projected my fears of dad onto Dick, casting him unconsciously in the role of an explosive tyrant.

I remember another childhood situation that affected me as an adult. We had an old car that could have been suitable for my sisters and me while learning to drive. Faced with this prospect of splitting an automobile three ways and the possibility of his never seeing it again himself, dad refused to teach us how to drive. I was an adult before I learned to handle an automobile.

Early in my marriage, a friend taught me how to drive. We went around and around the block, as I diligently practiced the complexities of brake and accelerator, steering wheel and direction. Finally, I set up two clothes poles in front of our house and practiced parallel parking for the driving test. A couple of days later I triumphantly returned home with my license!

We lived in an Akron suburb, and Dick refused to let me drive into town because of the heavy traffic. One day, while he was working, I sneaked a drive into town to pick up a new blender. The store was not on the main road, and traffic wouldn't be a problem.

My heart pounded and my knuckles turned white as I clutched the wheel and crept into town. Carefully, I eased into the parking lot, feeling only half-proud that I had made it—one way.

I picked up the blender, distractedly thanked the clerk, and hurried out to the car. Anxious to get the last leg of my journey over with, I opened the door, placed the package on the seat, eased behind the wheel, and turned the key. Nothing happened. Clicking the key back to "off," I tried again. Nothing.

What will I do now? What will Dick say?

I started experimenting. First this button, then that dial. Could it have something to do with the emergency brake? At last I hit on the solution. The car had an automatic transmission and would start only if the shift lever were in "park" position. I had left it in neutral.

I drove home, more confidently than before, but shaky

nevertheless. When Dick returned from work, I didn't mention the incident to him, even though my conscience nagged me a little.

"Did you happen to take the car to town today?" he asked casually later in the evening.

"No!" I sputtered, caught off guard. After taking two or three steps into the kitchen, I stopped to think. *Wait a minute. I won't live this way. I've got to tell him what happened.*

I slipped quietly back into the living room and sat beside him on the couch. "I have a confession to make . . ." Nervously, I began to relate my experience. I was sure that his reaction would be angry, as my father's would have been.

Instead he just smiled, "Good for you, Jeri. I'm glad you figured out what to do."

My problem was my preconceived ideas about how Dick would respond. I believed that I couldn't measure up. I sifted through everything he said, picking up evidence to support my suspicion, trying to prove his displeasure. If Dick said someone was a good cook, I decided he was disappointed in the dinner. I saddled my father's character on Dick's shoulders and, whenever Dick's response was not like my father's I was surprised. But happy relationships are based on reality. I had to learn that Dick was not my father.

Other pitfalls detoured and damaged our relationship, too. We often talked without revealing ourselves. Instead we chattered pointlessly—"What did you think of the Dodgers last night?" "What about that mess in the Middle East?" Through superficial communication, we learned *about* each other, but getting to *know* each other was illusive.

The purpose of communication is to create unity. Healthy communication skills are key elements in the flow of love. The "unholy trio"—hostility, fear, and guilt—keeps us from sharing ourselves with others, identifying with them, and they with us. Love requires that kind of sharing. Without it, relationships wither and die.

I knew that God's wisdom could help us resolve these difficulties. One day I was reminded of that when I turned to James 1:5: "If any of you lacks wisdom, let him ask of God, who gives to all men generously and without reproach, and it will be given to him."

"God," I prayed, "Give me the wisdom to know how to share my feelings with Dick, and then give me opportunities to use my new wisdom."

It took a misadventure on the freeway for me to learn the essence of one principle: sometimes we have to care enough to confront.

Even though I knew why the doctor wouldn't let Dick drive anymore, I hated my new job as chauffeur. It wasn't just the fact that more of my hours were being filled with extra responsibilities. Part of it was my discomfort with being Dick's driver. I had rarely driven with him as the passenger before the doctor's order, for Dick prided himself in being careful and safe. "If anything should happen, Jeri, I could think quicker than you could," he would say. Of course, I agreed.

It felt strange to have him sitting in "my" seat whenever we drove. It was like playing cat-and-mouse, trying to think of every move he would make—where he'd park, which lane he'd take, where to turn. I would attempt to make the right decision before he had a chance to tell me. But no matter how I tried, it was never right. If I parked in one place, he'd tell me to park in another. If I chose the left lane, he'd tell me to change to the right.

"Be careful, Jeri, there's another car beside you." "Jeri, there's a stop sign." "The light's red!"

After several weeks, my compassion for Dick began to vanish and my resentment of him grew. *Doesn't he know I can drive a car by myself? How does he think I manage when he's not with me?*

Dick had many driving rules. If, for example, anything was in the road, continue straight ahead. To swerve might endanger an unseen vehicle on either side.

On a clear, windy Southern California day, I was driving us home on the freeway after a long morning at the City of Hope. A wooden crate suddenly loomed in our lane. My first thought was "Don't swerve." I kept going. With a loud, nerve shattering crash, the box was demolished on impact. Both of us were weak with terror; I pulled over to the side immediately.

"Why on earth didn't you go around the box?" Dick barked, his face white.

Without answering, I drove on, dropping him off at home before I went to get the wheels re-aligned. The clanking of the dropped tools and the hiss of hydraulic racks punctuated my thoughts. As I watched the mechanics skillfully make the necessary adjustments, I knew I had to take a stand. The words, *I care enough to say what I have to say,* repeated themselves over and over in my mind.

After dinner that night I decided it was time for a confrontation. "Dick," I began timidly, but determined to finish. "Either you are going to drive the car or you're going to let me drive. I can't go on like this any longer. You tell me every move to make, and criticize me every second. That's going to stop!"

Dick sat tight-lipped and unresponsive as I chronicled my efforts toward independence.

"It's time for you to let me grow from a child into a woman," I chided. "If you do, I think you'll like the person you'll see."

"Are you through with me?" he demanded.

"Yes."

Feeble but furious, he grabbed his cane and limped out of the room, firmly closing the bedroom door behind him. There were tears in his eyes as he passed me.

Sadly I sat on the couch, wondering if I'd mishandled the situation. But less than a minute later he came back into the living room.

"I didn't realize what I was doing, Jeri." He spoke quietly, touching my face. "You're all I have. I need you . . . and I love you. He wrapped his arms around me and held me tenderly. I'd never felt closer to him.

From that moment on I began to feel free—and as if I'd grown six feet. Dick started to see me as a mature person. At last I felt equal to him.

The counseling process had helped me learn to communicate more effectively. Resentments we had erected through the years began to crumble under the impact of my willingness to share thoughts and feelings just as that box had been demolished from the impact of the car. Dick could see how much I wanted to help him through his illness, and he was becoming more confident that I was determined to remain with him and love him.

At times, that meant asserting myself in ways I had never thought possible. We decided to fly to Ohio for a few weeks during the summer. Dick had now been ill for three years. He was in such agony as he picked up the telephone to make our flight reservations, that I decided comfort was our prime concern.

"Dick, tell the ticket agent we want first class," I urged cheerfully.

"First class?" He scowled. "We've *never* flown first class!" His face twisted into a deep frown as he stiffened in his chair.

"I know. But I think you owe it to yourself to have the comfort."

"It costs a fortune!"

"Dick, you've worked hard for the money we have. Now is the time to enjoy it. I hate to say this, but you can't take it with you."

"Jeri, it's wasteful," Dick shot back, the level of his voice rising with each word. "We're not going first class!"

This is one time, Dick Krumroy, when I'm not going to be intimidated by your anger. "You either go first class," I blurted angrily, "or you go alone!"

Dick stared at me in shock. "You really mean that, don't you?"

"Yes, I do!" This assertiveness surprised me, although it felt good to be able to express myself so candidly.

He grumbled and muttered a good deal until the day

of our flight, but I was determined to hold firm. The extra leg room, the wheel chair that awaited him when we arrived at the terminal, the personal attention, and the delicious prime rib dinner calmed his spirits considerably.

"I'm glad we paid the extra money, Jeri," he confessed as we relaxed after the meal. "You were right. This *is* a lot better."

Although confronting him was frightening at times, our new-found freedom of expression was building a far better marriage. My only regret was that we had not sorted out the problems in our relationship long before this. My passive traits had remained hidden from me until responsibility forced them to the surface. I couldn't dwell on my regrets. Grief had taught us to communicate openly before it was too late.

8

Tattered Dreams and Broken Pieces

Tired, red-rimmed eyes stared back at me through the bedroom mirror. I looked old, haggard, sad.

Hours before, Dick had pleaded, "Honey, please—get a nurse for tonight."

Good luck! I thought, irritably. In the past three years, we had long since exhausted our list of private nurses.

Glancing at the corner of the mirror, my eyes rested on a Bible verse that I had taped there. "Don't be afraid," it read. "Just stand where you are and watch, and you will see the wonderful way the Lord will rescue you today" (Exodus 14:13 Living Bible).

I read the words, and reread them. A wave of anger hit me. "God! How can you say these things? If you loved us, you'd *do* something!"

I ripped the little verse into a thousand pieces and flung them, like colorless confetti, into the waste basket. Collapsing across my bed I sobbed, "Prove it, Lord . . . I don't believe it."

Almost immediately the phone rang. I choked back my tears and answered. It was Helen, a friend from our new church.

"Hi, Jeri," her cheery voice began. "I just wanted to find out how you're doing. I couldn't get you off my mind. How are you?"

"Not . . . so good," I sputtered. "I'll . . . I'll have to call you . . . back."

"Nice of her to call, but it's *not* enough," I muttered bitterly.

An hour later the ring of the door bell startled me. I peeked outside. There stood Helen, holding a large, bright chrysanthemum with a big plastic bumble bee on top. It almost looked real. Her husband, Chuck, stood beside her.

"Jeri, this flower is for *you,* not Dick," she whispered

and gave me a tight hug.

Tears fell again, for her words touched me deeply. Everyone always seemed to be praying for Dick, never for me. I'd often wondered if anyone undertood *my* pain in watching helplessly as Dick died slowly before my eyes.

Dick was too frail to stand to greet Chuck and Helen as they entered our living room.

"How are things, *really,* Dick?" Chuck's tone insisted upon an honest answer after the polite greetings were exchanged.

Dick and I looked at each other helplessly.

"Jeri's doing everything she can to make me comfortable, and I love her for it, but it's wearing her out." His voice sounded uneven. "She's so tired she can hardly move. Her arm got to hurting so bad she finally went to the doctor. It's bursitis. I feel terrible because there's not one thing I can do to make her life easier."

I had to look away from him. Once again the familiar burning began behind my eyelids—would I never run out of tears?

A new thought crowded into my consciousness. *Dick wants to give up living, but he doesn't know how.*

"I guess I feel guilty," Dick's voice sounded far away. "My sickness is making *her* sick. She does absolutely everything for me, and . . . "

"I'm just angry, that's all," I interrupted. Thinly veiled fury raised my voice unexpectedly. "I feel very frustrated and constantly angry. I don't understand why *we* have to be the ones going through all this. Our lives are nothing more than tattered dreams and broken pieces!"

"It must be hard to keep your emotions under control when you're so physically drained," Helen responded gently.

"Of course it is," I murmured. "It's a million times harder! There's no end in sight. Dick requires pain medication every two hours now. We're trying to find a nurse to relieve me a few nights a week. Every person we've called is either busy or doesn't want the job!"

Helen shrugged and shook her head sadly. "Well, I sure don't have all the answers. But I think we ought to pray together. God cares and knows your needs."

I rebelled at the seemingly useless ritual. *A lot of good this will do,* my mind grumbled. *I've done nothing but pray for three years and look where it's got me. God's got it all mapped out anyway. Why bother?*

Nevertheless I bowed my head while Chuck led in prayer.

I accepted this visit as God's way of showing me an awareness of my need. I appreciated Helen's love and concern, but the long, exhausting night was still ahead. I was to discover when God's Word says, "The Lord will rescue you today," it promises just that!

Chuck and Helen had been gone several hours when the phone rang.

"Jeri? Helen. Guess what? I found a nurse for you! She's coming to help you three nights a week. She's a Christian and won't accept a cent, so don't try to pay her. And Jeri, her father died of the same kind of cancer Dick has. She knows what to do."

At first I felt a wonderful sense of relief. A little later, though, with the lovely yellow flower Helen had brought fairly dazzling me from across the room, I felt guilty for having so many bad attitudes. No matter how often I shared my feelings with God, depression lingered. I was continually grappling with something—frustration or bitterness, fear or guilt.

My legs seemed to have weights in them, and even breathing was work. My arm was so painful that I had to have cortisone shots. I almost welcomed the injections—at least this was one area in which Dick didn't have to feel pain.

It didn't seem fair that Dick should have to do all the suffering, and I thought, *it's almost as if I can take some of the pain for him.* Then I'd scold myself for having such a ridiculous thought. It didn't relieve Dick's pain for me to suffer. Yet my guilty feelings lingered.

Dick felt guilty, too. Earlier that day he expressed his agony. "Jeri, I've searched my life over and over again. I can't figure out why. What did I do wrong that I've earned this much pain? I feel so helpless." Tears ran quietly down his cheeks, and he didn't bother to wipe them away.

"Oh, honey!" I cried. "God's not punishing you!"

We both knew that sin must be paid for, but we were confident as Christians that Jesus had suffered on the cross for us. Why, then, does God allow such horrible trials to enter our lives? I had long since lost my ability to search the scriptures for guidance. The pages seemed cold and empty before my eyes. Night after night I listened to tapes of Bible passages, and my subconscious was absorbing all that I heard. Slowly I began to find answers to some of my immediate questions. The answer I found was that God uses adversity in our lives much the same way athletes undergo rigorous training in preparation for competition.

> Endure hardship as discipline; God is treating you as sons . . . Moreover, we have all had human fathers who disciplined us and we respected them for it. How much more should we submit to the Father of our spirits and live! Our fathers disciplined us for a little while as they thought best; but God disciplines us for our good, that we may share in his holiness. No discipline seems pleasant at the time, but painful. Later on, however, it produces a harvest of righteousness and peace for those who have been trained by it.
>
> Hebrews 12:7, 9-11 (NIV)

In the light of this passage, I realized that discipline is not a punitive action—it is an educational one. It is training and preparation. But for what?

> Consider it pure joy, my brothers, whenever you face trials of many kinds, because you know that the testing of your faith develops perseverance. Perseverance must finish its work so that you may be mature and complete, lacking nothing.
>
> James 1:2-4 (NIV)

Trials make us whole; adversity enables us to die. I realized that Dick and I had to come to this point before God could use us fully. If we're dead to "self," God is more able to live through us, pouring vitality into our empty vessels.

Another passage gave me much comfort, for it expresses God's purpose for us all:

> We know that in all things God works for the good of those who love him, who have been called according to his purpose. For those God foreknew he also predestined to be conformed to the likeness of his Son, that he might be the firstborn among many brothers.
>
> Romans 8:28, 29 (NIV)

Well, then, did God send cancer to conform Dick and me to this image? Does God sit in heaven handing out tragedies—cancer to Dick, muscular dystrophy to another, paralysis to someone else?

No! These things come because we live in a world where disease exists. We are human, therefore, we know death. Yet through Jesus, we can receive life. Out of the broken lumber of our lives God builds a foundation that enables us to be more like Jesus.

It was hard for me to submit to this painful and exhausting training. Jesus understands this, for at Gethsemane he also agonized with the problem of submission.

"My Father," he cried, "if it is possible, let this cup pass from me . . . " Jesus didn't enjoy pain any more than I. He had witnessed the cruelty of Roman crucifixion before, and heard the agonizing screams of the dying. Jesus had such a sense of union with God that, in the end, he was able to say, "If this cannot pass away unless I drink it, thy will be done" (Matthew 26:39, 42). His was a true act of submission.

In contrast, our ordeal exposed my willful attitude toward God whose plan was to take Dick home, but I had fought this at every turn. Expecting God to make things easy for me, I reacted with bitterness when our suffering increased. I did not have a balanced perspective on my union with God, and therefore it was difficult to see a plan for our lives.

I was reminded of an important letter a friend once received. By some misfortune, it was torn into pieces. Determined to read it, she stayed up most of the night putting the letter back together. It took hours, and by the time she had every scrap in place, my friend was too exhausted to read what it said. When she awakened the next morning, the message made perfect sense to her.

So it was with me. I couldn't understand all that was going on in our lives because I was only looking at shredded pieces. My fatigue even kept me from seeing *them* clearly. I felt torn, but though I didn't know it at the time, God was putting together the scraps of my life. Jeremiah once had this to say about God's role in our tattered lives:

> "I know the plans I have for you," declares the Lord, "plans to prosper you and not to harm you, plans to give you hope and a future. Then you will call upon me and come and pray to me, and I will listen to you.
> "You will seek me and find me when you seek me with all your heart. I will be found by you," declares the Lord, "and will bring you back from captivity . . . "
> Jeremiah 29:11–14 (NIV)

Even though I doubted God's plan for me, I was sorting through the small pieces of the pattern. I held on to the promise that as I let God's Word lead me, the jigsaw of life would one day fit together.

9
Equal Ground

You've tricked me again! Startled, I looked around. *Where did that thought come from?*

Returning from the hospital one rain-soaked afternoon, I pulled into our driveway and garage. "Go ahead and go in," I mumbled to Dick. "I'll bring your things."

I watched his withered body disappear into the warm house. "Home again, home again, home again." The windshield wipers mocked me with their useless, squeaky efforts. Turning them off in disgust, I sat motionless in the car. The thought, *You've tricked me again,* flashed in my mind. What did it mean?

My mind raced as I gathered Dick's belongings. *I thought he was gone this time. God, I was ready for you to take him, and you didn't. How many times more, God?* Shaking my head, I tried to counter those thoughts. *How can you think such a terrible thing? He's rallied! He's come back! You should be rejoicing.*

"I'm sorry, God," I sighed. "He's yours—and you have the right to do what you want with him—and with me. Help me not to be anxious. Help me to keep going."

I had prepared myself for Dick's death so often, only to have him rally enough to come home. The trouble was, his pain worsened, his problems increased, and I grew wearier every moment. I struggled with ambivalent emotions because I didn't want my husband to die, yet I didn't want this incredible suffering to continue any more.

That night Dick stepped out of the shower and caught a glimpse of himself in the steamy mirror. He stopped, aghast. "I look like an accordion," he murmured.

It was an apt description of his body for, as the vertebrae in his midsection collapsed, he appeared to be folding up. He wasn't the least bit fat, but overlapping folds of skin layered on top of each other around his midsection.

Dick grabbed the largest towel he could find and wrapped it around himself. Carefully, he stepped out of the bathroom, sat down on the bed, buried his head in his hands, and began to shake with great, silent sobs.

I ran to his side and sat down, placing my arm gently around his shoulders.

"What's wrong, honey?" I asked.

"I just saw myself in the mirror." His voice was hoarse. "How in the world could you love me this way?"

I tightened my hug slightly, careful not to cause too much pressure. We sat there for a few minutes. The lump in my throat kept me silent, and I tried to swallow it away. Slowly, our eyes met. As sick as he was, his eyes were clear and deep, and when I looked into them I saw the real Dick Krumroy.

"Dick, your body *is* deteriorating. But you are more than skin and blood and muscle and bone to me. You are still very much the man I married, and I will always love you." We cried in each other's arms.

"It would be such a relief to you if I were to die," he muttered.

"Honey, if God took you home tonight, I would be glad that you are free from all this agony. But I'm never going to be glad to say goodbye to you."

Later that night I got up to get Dick his morphine. After I'd given him the painful injections, he sighed cautiously, "Jeri, do you think you could sleep in the guest bedroom from now on?"

I stood there in silence, trying to gather my thoughts. "You don't want me to sleep with you anymore?" I choked.

"It isn't that I don't want you," Dick groaned. "It's just that even the slightest movement is torture for me. I know you're not sleeping well, either."

"No. I guess I'm not. Lots of times I sense that you're awake."

"When I can't sleep I can keep the television on for diversion, and work on my needlepoint. I want to have these two finished at Christmas for Karin and for Lonnie and

Bob's new baby."

"I think it would probably be good for me to sleep in the guest room, then. You can call me if you need me." I kissed him goodnight and stepped into the other room.

Tears trickled down my cheeks as I lay by myself in the dark. I knew the extent of Dick's pain, and that he didn't love me any less. Yet I had an overwhelming feeling of rejection. This was one more step in the gradual winding-down of our physical relationship.

It had been nearly eight months since we were able to enjoy each other intimately. Dick felt guilty, and thought he was failing me. He even asked the doctor to provide some medication to help. There was nothing they could do to eliminate the impotency, and Dick was crushed.

"Jeri, I'm cheating you of a normal life. You have needs I can't meet, and . . . " He broke down, and we had sat together sobbing. Now I couldn't even share the closeness of our bed with him ever again.

"This isn't fair, God. Why are you doing this to me?" I agonized. "What is life all about, anyway? I miss the closeness of our marriage. You may be preparing me for Dick's going, but it hurts . . . it really hurts."

In times like these, rationalizations are of no comfort. Recognizing that God was preparing me for our final days together didn't help. The hurt was so deep that I felt rejected and unloved, although my head told me it wasn't true; my heart told my head it was.

There is no time in a person's life that affection becomes more priceless, more vital, more necessary than when the end of life is in sight. Yet here we were—unable even to touch each other. Pain stood between Dick and me like a jealous third party, keeping us apart. We could hold hands to pray, and we prayed together every night, but that was of little comfort to me.

Throughout our marriage, Dick had always been tenderly affectionate. In church he would slip his hand over mine or put his arm protectively around me. He never failed each day to tell me he loved me and to demonstrate his love and affection in a physical way.

Gradually we discovered new and precious ways to express ourselves. We filled the void in our hearts with smiles, gently-held hands, whispered endearments. Dick began to send me romantic greeting cards, writing intimate things to express in words what he could no longer say with gestures.

Frequently he would surprise me with gift-wrapped boxes of love, or flowers. When Dick could no longer shop on his own, he would ask a woman-friend of ours to do it for him.

Yet I continued to struggle with my frustration and feelings of rejection, and with my disappointment in God for letting all this happen.

One afternoon while Dick was in the hospital again, I was waiting in the main lobby as the technicians worked with him. I'd been idly thumbing through a magazine, when I noticed a gentleman sitting across from me.

"Hi," he nodded.

"Hi!" I smiled at him. "Is someone in your family here?"

"No, I've come to visit a close friend. He's critically ill."

We chatted for about fifteen minutes.

"My husband's dying from cancer," I finally confided.

"Oh, I'm sorry." He spoke understandingly, and I nodded. "I know what you're going through. My wife died of cancer, too." His voice seemed to fade as the memory of his own pain returned.

He shared feelings about his own grief and told me a little about his adjustment since his wife's death.

As we talked, I found comfort in what he was saying. His words and tone reflected the intensity of his suffering. He had felt what I was feeling.

We ran into each other several times that week, shared coffee in the coffee shop, and visited. I found myself more and more attracted to him. Deeply disturbed and frightened by my pounding heart, I wondered, *why can't I control my emotions?*

A void clearly existed that Dick couldn't fill. It didn't help matters, either, when the man admitted that he was attracted to *me*. To me? I was, all at the same time, flattered, flustered, and frightened. There I was, a married woman, actually feeling attracted to a man who wasn't my husband. This had *never* happened to me before.

My feelings of guilt were so overwhelming that I rushed to Dr. Wagner on the verge of panic.

"What's happening to me? Why do I feel this way?" I almost wept.

"Jeri," Dr. Wagner smiled. "You're so very human!"

"Yes, but I'm married."

"You *are,* very much married, and you don't have the right to give in to these feelings. But what you've experienced is normal. You're allowing a natural emotion to torment you when it is the *expression* of that feeling that would determine your guilt. You did not submit to your temptation, and no wrong was committed."

Through this experience, new words of devotion to Dick—and to God—found their way into my journal: *Before you say goodbye, you remain faithful.*

Together Dr. Wagner and I tried to deal with my intense negative reaction to sleeping in the guest room. Slowly I began to realize that my feelings were triggered by another childhood memory. Mother and dad had always slept in different rooms. I never understood why dad slept in the attic and mother on the second floor, but I sensed rejection in their lack of marital closeness. My move to the guest room made me feel rejected and unloved, too.

More early influences were bringing to the surface other destructive emotions in me—especially guilt. My conscience troubled me frequently over what seemed to be an endless parade of personal shortcomings. I felt guilty for enjoying fleeting moments of happiness—it seemed wrong, somehow, to linger over a second cup of coffee in the morning. I felt guilty when my bursitis responded to the cortisone shot, giving me a measure of relief from the pain, while Dick's morphine wasn't helping him that much. When

I stole a few moments of rest in the afternoon, I had the uneasy feeling there was something I really should be doing. I felt like driving into the sunset—running, running away. But where? Dick needed me. What if it were me? I felt guilty when I didn't want to visit Dick in the hospital, when I wanted to rush from his room and hide from his hideous illness, when I couldn't control my hours of depression, when it seemed as though I wasn't trusting God enough.

And then there was the matter of the cleaning woman. I had hired a woman to help out with the household chores. Exhausted, and crippled by bursitis, I simply had to have some rest. Dick encouraged me to hire her, yet every time she bustled through the front door, I tried and convicted myself in a court of one.

With Dr. Wagner's help, I began to understand why. He helped me remember another scene from my childhood. I saw mother stretched out leisurely on the couch while our cleaning woman worked busily in the kitchen, singing as she scrubbed. The front door slammed—father was home! There was tension visible immediately, for he could not disguise his annoyance. Mother was spending *his* hard-earned cash for a maid, when she should have been doing the work herself. In my family, the harder we worked, the more we felt loved. Allowing someone else to do "our" work made us feel guilty.

"This shows how guilt can come when we don't live up to the expectations of others, Jeri," Dr. Wagner explained. "Adult conscience pangs often come because we haven't transferred authority from our parents to God. It's common to see adults trying to impress their parents with good conduct. The parent's death can exaggerate these pangs, for parental approval is no longer possible.

"But God's favor is all that counts. God offers freedom from the invisible parent-figure who silently chided you for behavior that was unacceptable when you were a child. It is liberating to know God in a parent relationship. We must measure up only to this standard."

Forgiveness is another enduring liberator. With Dr. Wagner I discovered that talking out our feelings can expose the basis of our guilt, but forgiveness is the eraser that wipes the slate clean. We have God's promise on this: "If we confess our sins, He is faithful and righteous to forgive . . . and to cleanse us from all unrighteousness" (1 John 1:9).

God has designed an intricate balance in our emotions. Our Maker's mercy can absolve us from the guilt of sin, but the cleansing is incomplete until we release ourselves. Self-inflicted guilt is the hardest to forgive because the responsibility is ours alone. The road to recovery lies in our willingness to forget the past. The Apostle Paul wrote to the Philippians . . . forgetting what is behind and straining toward what is ahead, I press on toward the goal to win the prize for which God has called me heavenward in Christ Jesus (3:13, 14, NIV).

A few weeks after I had resolved my emotional and physical temptations and stopped feeling guilty about them, it was time for Dick to have another checkup at the City of Hope. A new nurse greeted us cheerfully. Glancing over the records for a moment, she suddenly looked up.

"How tall are you?"

"Six-foot, two," Dick replied automatically.

She looked blank for a moment, then laughed. "Oh, you're kidding! You couldn't possibly be six-foot, two!"

Her bright manner softened the insensitivity of her words. But my heart sank.

"I'm going to measure you," she announced, determined to mark the correct height in the little blank.

The scale was in the main hallway, where doctors, nurses, and orderlies hurried about their chores. Meekly Dick stepped up onto the black platform. The nurse slipped the chrome height measure down until the arm rested on Dick's thin grey hair.

"That's what I thought! You're only five-foot, eight!"

A look of dismay and dejection saddened Dick's face. "Are you sure? I can't be!" His voice sharpened with disbelief. "Check it again," he demanded.

"Five-foot, eight," she repeated, carefully recording the new information.

My thoughts went back unexpectedly to our wedding day. I had wondered if Dick was too tall for me. There was a twelve inch difference in our heights.

"Dick . . . " I groped for the right words, trying to be cheerful."Maybe God is putting us on equal ground. Now you can't be looking down on me all the time."

I glanced at him, and saw a flicker of a smile. We both knew that I had grown a little taller, had learned to stand a little straighter in the past painful months. It wouldn't be long before I would reach and stretch higher and farther than either of us could imagine.

10

Strength to Survive

Summer melted into autumn of the third year of Dick's illness and the days dragged on. An uncertain time frame existed for us. Life and death seemed forever at war. Endless questions filled endless days.

How long will Dick suffer? How am I going to manage practical things? Will I be able to make wise decisions? Is there anything else I can do to ease Dick's agony? What do I do if he dies at home? Should I tell him the cancer has spread?

Besides the endless questions, the pain of watching Dick suffer intensified, creating the most difficult kind of grief. It went on and on, with glimmers of hope making the pain all the more piercing.

I found that my physical setting was affecting my outlook. I was forever in a triangle: home, office, hospital. Dick was aware of this problem, too, for he was trapped in the same pattern. It had been some time since he had been able to work at the Foundation on a regular basis. Although we were able to go to church every week, we needed to change our routine and surroundings on occasion. It was especially important for me to do something for myself, and Dick realized this before I did.

"Why don't you plan a day and go shopping?" he would urge, or, "Why don't you invite someone to go to lunch?" One day he said, "Honey, I think some exercise would do you good."

"Probably," I murmured absently. "I do a lot of sitting. No time, though."

"Well, I want you to *make* time. I had Eleanor pick up this information for me." He handed me a brochure featuring a health spa.

"Oh, no, Dick. I have too much to do. This is too expensive for the amount of time I could use it." But his disappointed expression told me that at times receiving is as important as giving. This time I needed to be a gracious recipient.

In truth I was delighted. I loved to exercise, and the sauna took away the tension in my over-tired body. I looked forward to that hour and a half each week when I did something for me. I'd return from the spa relaxed and refreshed, but *always* on call.

Dick needed a change of scenery, too. When he suggested at the end of September that we take a weekend vacation, I quickly agreed.

"Where should we go?" I asked.

"To the redwoods."

"That's too far, Dick."

"Not if we go to Sequoia. Libbie and Jim can go with us. They have a friend with a cabin at Hume Lake, and he said we could use it for the weekend. What do you say?"

"Sounds wonderful," I laughed.

Jim drove us in his car, and I had him pull over several times so I could give Dick his morphine, His skin was like leather, and there were few spots left on his body for the injections. In spite of his pain, Dick handled the trip well.

It was raining when we arrived at the cabin, but it didn't matter. The air was fresh and inviting, and the forest fragrances caressed our noses. The cottage had a huge fireplace, so Jim and I gathered wood and built a big fire while Libbie made hot chocolate for us. We roasted marshmallows that evening and talked late into the night.

The next day we drove into King's Canyon. There were lots of hairpin curves, but Jim's careful driving, taking it easy on every sharp turn, protected Dick from sudden jolts. I was touched by Jim's thoughtfulness and concern for Dick. The forest called to us as we drove, and we saw deer, a bear, and multitudes of stellar jays.

That night we stayed in a town about 240 miles from home, and arrived back at 3:30 the next afternoon. I was delighted that Dick had enough energy left and the appetite to go out for a fish supper. He seemed so well that I thought, *This has all been a bad dream. Truly I won't lose him after all.*

The next morning Dick was in agony. His face was pale, and I wondered if he needed blood again. I drove him back to the hospital.

"How are you doing, Dick?" the doctor asked cheerfully.

"I'm getting better, Doc." Dick was giving his standard answer, and it infuriated me. Then, noticing my grim expression, he confessed, "Well, I guess I'm not as good as I'd like to be. I—I'm about ready to throw in the towel."

"Dick, I want you to try some more chemotherapy."

"Doc, that will only make me sick. I'll give it a try, but we both know it won't cut the pain."

The following day I picked up the mail on my way out the door to visit Dick at the hospital. *Hmm. A letter from Dick's mother.* I stopped long enough to scan the note.

I sighed heavily. Dick's sister, Mildred, had been diagnosed in June as having cancer—lymphoma. Mother Krumroy's letter said she was failing rapidly.

"Dick, Mildred's not doing very well," I explained gently. "She's back in the hospital, too. But your mom says she's not having any pain."

Dick shook his head sadly. "Why does this happen? What *causes* this, Jeri? Dear God, please help them find a cure for this before Bob and Janie are our age." We sat silently for a few minutes. "I just had a terrible thought," he confessed suddenly.

"What is it?"

"I'm going to be angry if Mildred dies before I do. I've been hanging on now for over three years."

"So will I," I whispered.

Dick searched my face suspiciously. "You know, don't you, that you're going to have all sorts of men knocking at your door."

"What?" I was stunned.

"I don't see how you could possibly remarry."

"Remarry? Dick, whatever gave you such an idea?"

"How could anybody ever fall in love with someone else?"

"Dick, no one's ever going to be able to take your place!" I could sense Dick's anger and frustration, and I really couldn't blame him for his feelings. No one wants to think of himself as replaceable.

"You're going to be lonely, Jeri," Dick continued. "You can't rush into something out of loneliness. You need to be careful."

"Dick, if I ever do remarry, I'll be very careful to choose wisely," I interrupted. "The Holy Spirit is the Good Counselor. God will guide me, Dick."

It hurt me to realize that Dick thought me incapable of being wise and selective, although I shouldn't have been surprised, considering the length of time I had been dependent upon him.

"One thing—he'd *better* take good care of you," he threatened.

And just how do you think you're going to see to that? I wondered. Now my anger and frustration were equal to his.

"That's enough, Dick. I have no intention of running out and replacing you like a . . . furnace filter. I don't want you to talk about remarriage anymore. I'm going to get a cup of tea."

I strode out of the room and leaned against the wall in the hallway. Dick meant more to me than anyone on earth. How *could* he decide I'd want to remarry? Yet I know that people often rush into new relationships too soon after a death. I resolved to take my time, no matter how lonely I felt.

When I returned to Dick's room, he was working on his needlepoint. "Home is where the heart is," it read.

"This is going to be yours, honey. Jeri . . ." he paused, collected his thoughts, and spoke softly. "I would feel guilty if what I said were to keep you from happiness."

It was a relief to me that he would sanction my remarriage if I ever chose to do it, but I never found out what had caused him such anxiety about it. I kissed him gently on the forehead.

"Honey, yesterday I asked the doctor what would happen if I stopped taking the transfusions."

"What did he say?" I tried to hide my uneasiness.

"He said I'd fail rapidly—maybe within a few weeks."

We said nothing for several minutes. *God, you'll have to tell him to give up those transfusions if that's what your plan is. I cannot urge him to stop, but neither will I ask him to continue.* Before our little trip, the doctor had taken me aside to tell me Dick was full of cancer now. His pain would soon be almost impossible to endure.

"Jeri? Are you afraid for your future?"

For a moment I couldn't answer. *Dick, I'm terrified. But I can't let you know that; it wouldn't be good for you to have to deal with it.* I chose my words carefully.

"It's impossible to imagine what life will be without you. We've been married more than half my life, and sometimes I wish my life would end when yours does. At first I was convinced that I couldn't make it, but the counseling sessions are helping me to work out my feelings, and his counseling is giving me confidence in myself."

Driving home on the freeway that night, blinded with tears, I found myself in the wrong lane for my exit. I zoomed around the car in front of me and swerved into the right lane. Suddenly I saw a red light blinking behind me. I pulled over and stopped.

"Lady, do you know what you did?"

I burst into tears. "No officer, I really don't. I guess my mind was somewhere else. My husband is in the hospital. He's dying." I leaned my head against the steering wheel and sobbed.

The officer waited a moment, and then spoke gently. "I am really sorry, ma'am. You can't drive like this, though. You won't help your husband by causing an accident. I'm sorry," he repeated, "but I still have to give you a ticket."

"Thank you," I mumbled. Then I wondered why I should thank him. Yet I knew that I needed to be more careful, even if my heart was broken. I still had to obey the law.

I had found myself lost several times on the wrong freeway because of the numbness I felt when leaving the hospital. This was God's way of helping me see my obligation, of protecting me from injury.

At home I climbed into the shower. The steaming water felt good, and I let it run down my back for a long time. I put my face into the spray, relishing its freshness. Finally I turned the water off and pushed the door. It wouldn't budge. I pushed harder. Nothing.

"Get me out of here!" I cried. "God, you can't do this to me!" I banged on the door of the shower and began to cry. "You know what I'm going through. You shouldn't let this happen." I struggled and wrestled, trying to pry the door open.

"What have I done to deserve this?" I cried angrily. "Haven't I been through enough without this? God, you've *got* to get me out."

Finally I sat in the corner and wrapped my arms around myself, and prayed. "Please, God, help me somehow to find my way out. If you do, I promise I'll work harder at not complaining."

Wild ideas fluttered through my head like half-crazed butterflies. I could put my foot in the drain and float out the top. No, then I'd have to drop seven feet down the other side. Besides, if I left the water on, I'd look like a prune. I could imagine the newspaper headlines: *Naked woman starves to death in shower; Water company insists thousand dollar bill must be paid.*

Saner thoughts crept into my head. "God, if you could give David strength to kill Goliath, couldn't you please give me the strength to get out of here? I'm tired. And I'm cold!"

Somehow, with one mighty effort, I lifted the glass door out of its groove, slipped out the side, and placed the door in the shower after struggling for nearly an hour. Wrapping my towel around me, I stumbled into the bedroom and fell, exhausted, onto the bed feeling like small, wounded child, wanting to be held and comforted. I wept with relief.

The next morning I fixed myself breakfast and reflected on my experience. What I had gone through in the shower was a grief process in miniature: denial, anger, bargaining, depression, and finally, acceptance of my situation. But I had been victorious! The door moved and I was free.

I turned on my tape recorder to listen to a chapter from Philippians. One verse stood out as if it were being emphasized especially for me: "I can do all things through Christ which strengtheneth me." (Philippians 4:13, KJV).

Later, when I tried to replace the door in the groove, I couldn't even move it. God *had* come to my rescue. *I will survive this ordeal,* I told myself, *and I will be the better for it because God will be my strength.*

11

The Big Decision

"Sweetheart, go ask Roy for some help with this," Dick pleaded.

"All right," I finally sighed. "I'll be back in a few minutes, honey." I rubbed my aching arm, put on a sweater, and stepped slowly out the front door headed toward our neighbor's.

Dick's doctor had suggested he wear stretch socks to minimize the threat of blood clots. Because of his back, Dick couldn't bend to put them on, and I'd been helping him. It was like working on a dead log to get a size thirteen stretch sock up to his thigh.

The bursitis in my arm had worsened. It was all I could do to give Dick his injections. Even two cobalt treatments hadn't helped me, and my pain intensified daily. Finally, Dick asked me to get help. I explained the situation to Roy, adding, "I really hate to ask you to do this."

"I'd be *happy* to help with Dick's socks, Jeri." His eyes glistened, and his voice echoed genuine pleasure at the opportunity to do something for us. After that he stopped by every morning for fifteen minutes before he went to work.

He always came to the door with a smile, and before long a special bond developed between the men. They visited together and prayed for each other. I was glad Dick had someone with whom he could share his feelings. Roy was so gentle and engaging as he worked that Dick even seemed to forget that he was being dressed by another man.

One crisp October noontime I hurried home to give Dick his morphine and to entice him to eat some lunch. He had almost no appetite, and most food didn't even taste good to him. Often I wandered the aisles of the supermarket in a daze trying to figure out what to prepare for him.

"Hi, sweetheart! How about a cheese sandwich and a malt?"

"Mildred died this morning. I just got the phone call a few minutes ago," he sighed sullenly.

This isn't fair, God, I raged. *How can you let Dick suffer on and on like this, and take his sister so quickly? How much worse does he have to get?*

Dick *was* worsening. The pressure in his chest was so intense that he slept sitting up most of the time. He went to the Foundation only to visit. When he did go, I often took him to my office to give him his morphine. His trips to the hospital were occurring weekly now, and it was the frequent blood transfusions that were keeping him alive.

"Oh, Jeri, I wish I could die," Dick whispered.

I took his hand and we sat silently together. *I know,* I kept thinking, *I know.*

"How does anyone just give up and die?" he agonized.

You give up the transfusions, Dick. I cannot tell you that. It can only be your decision.

Over the next several days Dick and I alternated between anger and sorrow over Mildred's death. We were sorrowful that she was gone. We were angry too at the senselessness of the hideous disease that took her life and was eating away at Dick's. There didn't seem to be a bright spot anywhere in our lives.

Then one day I came home from the spa to a jubilant Dick.

"Jeri! Janie just called. Guess what?" Dick was grinning broadly, and his eyes twinkled. "She and Randy are bringing little Karin for a visit."

"When?" My mind raced with the plans I'd have to make . . . meals and a place for everyone to sleep. Although Janie would be a big help to me, and it would be wonderful to be together, I'd still need to make some arrangements.

"Monday! Isn't it great?" Dick leaned slowly back in his chair and smiled with satisfaction. I knew he was thinking about our beautiful little granddaughter. When they arrived, at nine months old and just beginning to walk, Karin charmed us completely. It was hard for me to keep from cuddling her every moment. I took her to work with me one afternoon, and she was the center attraction.

For Dick the visit was a bittersweet one. He longed to hold Karin, to bounce her on his knee and play piggy back with her. Limited in his movement, he could only reach out and caress her hair or touch her hand, and often his eyes brimmed with tears as he watched her. I left the room often to keep from crying in front of Dick. How sad that he wouldn't be able to be here to watch her grow up.

During the nights, when Janie got up to care for Karin, she and Dick would talk. Once when I got up to give Dick his morphine, I heard scraps of their conversation.

"You and Bob are able to face the world," Dick was saying. "Remember that time you changed the tire for us when we were on vacation?"

Janie murmured something, and they laughed.

"Please look out for mom," Dick pleaded. "She'll be so lonely out here. She's always been so dependent on me that it will be hard for her to go on." There was a short silence, and I heard Dick sigh with pain. "I'll have to wake mom up pretty soon to give me another shot, I guess. This is so hard, lying around waiting between shots."

I leaned against the refrigerator door letting the tears trickle down my face. Janie was speaking soothingly to Dick, but I couldn't hear it. I chided myself for listening.

"Dick," I called out softly, "I'm fixing your shot." After Janie went back to bed, I sat with Dick for a little while.

"She's quite a girl," he bragged.

"She's your daughter. That must have a lot to do with it," I agreed.

"Jeri, I'm not going to the airport with you tomorrow."

"Are you in too much pain?"

"No more than usual. It's just that this may be the last time I'll ever see Janie and Randy and Karin. I don't want our final goodbye to be at an airport. I just couldn't stand that." Dick put his head in his hands and wept softly.

A week or so after Janie's family left, the phone rang.

"Mom!" Bob's voice was brimming with excitement. "It's a boy! We've named him Ryan Richard—after dad."

"Oh, Bob! I'm so happy for you. Is Lonnie all right?"

"Fantastic! She did really well, mom. Ryan is so tiny and beautiful. Listen, we're going to come for Thanksgiving. Ryan will be six weeks old by then, and Lonnie will be able to travel."

"Bob, that would be wonderful." It felt so good to smile and to have something to rejoice about. *Please, God, let Dick live long enough to see little Ryan.*

Dick was eager to see his new grandson and visit with our son and daughter-in-law. I could tell that he was putting forth every effort to stay out of the hospital. Yet his pain was almost unbearable, and he was exhausted.

"How do you give up and die, Jeri?" he asked again. I bit my lip and shook my head. I couldn't say anything. I hated this ordeal. I'd been begging God to release Dick from his misery, although facing life alone seemed like crossing a dark, empty chasm.

I was finally beginning to realize that if Dick couldn't stay with me unless he suffered, I was willing for him to go. "Lord," I prayed, "why should he prolong his suffering just to be with me? Whisper to Dick the words I couldn't say."

On a day early in November, Dick said, "Jeri, I was planning to keep our office building in Akron. I thought it would be a good source of income for you. The more I think about it, the more convinced I am that it would be a problem for you. I'm going to put it up for sale, and when it sells, I'll be ready to go."

Several days later we went to the hospital for the results of the most recent blood tests. The doctor thumbed gloomily through the report.

"Well, Dick," his somber voice broke the silence. "It looks as if you need another transfusion."

"Doctor," I began hesitantly, "Dick asked me the other day, 'How do you give up and die?' I didn't have an answer. What would you have said?"

The doctor gazed thoughtfully for a moment at my husband. "Dick, have the transfusions helped your pain?"

Dick shook his head.

"You know that they provide you with red cells to carry oxygen and nutrients throughout your body. Without the transfusions, your blood count goes down and you weaken. When it drops too low, you won't be able to rally."

"No." Dick responded slowly, his voice trembling and his face a mirror of dread. "I don't believe I'll be having any more transfusions."

"I can't blame you." The doctor reached compassionately for Dick's hand. "I think we're all better off facing reality together, and you're both wise to be able to talk this out. Some couples never can face death together, and it's awfully hard on the surviving spouse. Very well, then, Dick. No more transfusions. I'll do everything I can to save you from suffering."

That was Dick's big decision. It was a hard one, but he had made it himself. I admired him for it, although I could hardly bear to think of the consequences. It seemed as if he had just signed his own death warrant.

The following week I wandered into his room to find him sitting on the edge of his bed, staring into space.

"Dick? Are you all right?" I asked tenderly.

"Jeri . . ." Dick paused, his eyes avoiding mine. "Jeri, I think the Lord just spoke to me."

"What did God say?"

"God told me I . . . I won't be here for Christmas."

Holding hands tightly, we looked silently into each other's eyes. Tears streamed down our cheeks. Christmas was just weeks away.

Two days before Thanksgiving, Bob phoned.

"How's dad?"

I glanced at Dick. His face was contorted.

"We're looking forward to your visit tomorrow, Bob."

"He's worse, then?"

"Yes."

"Mom," Bob's voice sounded troubled. "Lonnie's sick. It's her appendix. I had to rush her to the hospital for emergency surgery. I'm afraid we can't come now. It'll be another six weeks or so before Lonnie can travel."

"Oh, Bob, I'm so sorry. Is she okay now? Who's taking

care of Ryan?"

"She's fine—Lonnie's mom is helping."

Dick asked to talk with Bob, and while they chatted I paced the kitchen floor. I doubted that Dick would be able to handle a visit six weeks from now. If he had heard the Lord correctly, he wouldn't be with us.

"I'm disappointed," Dick reflected sadly. "I was hoping they could come. I really wanted to see my little grandson. Thanksgiving will be lonely without them."

"Me, too. Honey, I have to run over to Roy and Mary's for a few minutes. I promised her my Cranberry Waldorf recipe." I threw my coat over my shoulders and went over to the Andersons'.

"Mary, I need to call our son, and I don't want Dick to overhear. Could I use your phone?"

"Of course, Jeri." Mary ushered me into their family room closing the door so I could have privacy. I dialed Bob's number carefully.

"Bob, this is mom. I couldn't talk to you because dad was right there. He's failing rapidly. I think you'd better come as soon as Lonnie can get along okay by herself."

"It's that bad?" Bob's voice trembled.

"I'm afraid so, son."

"I'll leave Lonnie with her mother and be there Saturday afternoon. Don't worry, mom."

It was the dreariest Thanksgiving of our lives. I don't remember what the weather was like. We were in the pit of sorrow, and even if the day had been crisp, clear and bright like most Southern California Thanksgivings, I wouldn't have noticed. Everything about that week seemed dark and overcast.

Dick spent the day in bed, watching all of the football games. I didn't bother to cook anything because even the smell of cooking food made Dick nauseous. I'd set up a small grill in the garage to cook for myself out there. A milk shake with an egg mixed in for protein was the only thing Dick could tolerate.

Late in the afternoon a friend dropped by to visit with

Dick and to bring me a turkey sandwich and some pumpkin pie. While he visited with Dick, I went for a walk.

"God, I know you're going to take Dick home soon. Help me to be thankful for all the wonderful years we had together, and to be grateful when you take him that he's no longer in pain. Next year, Lord, I don't want to spend Thanksgiving here alone. Help me to plan something—to be with people."

I leaned against a tree and inhaled the damp autumn air. The heaviness of my grief made me want to fall into a deep, silent, endless sleep.

Saturday afternoon I drove to pick up Bob after his flight arrived.

"Bob, I want you to be prepared for dad. He's quite thin, now, because he can't eat. His back has collapsed so much that he's lost about six inches in height. The morphine keeps him sluggish, so when he's sitting down, he can't keep his eyes open. He's given up the transfusions. I think we'll have to take him to the hospital tomorrow."

"Do you think this is the end, mom?"

"I just don't know. It's seemed like the end so many times before, but I've ended up taking him home again. This time there are no transfusions to help him rally. This could be it. But I don't want to say it."

"In a way, mom, you've been through almost as much as he has, haven't you?"

I nodded. "Bob, I think I've experienced every emotion there is. If I hadn't been able to get professional help, I don't think I would have made it. Dr. Wagner has helped me deal with all of this, but I don't think I'll ever be able to put into words what I've felt. I never knew I *had* so many emotions."

I left Dick and Bob at home alone for several hours. I never asked what they talked about but, when I returned, Bob's expression told me he knew his father was going to die soon.

None of us spoke as Bob drove us to the hospital the next day. While the nurse prepared a new medical history on Dick, Bob and I had about an hour for lunch. Later, as we walked across the parking lot, we met a mother and her twenty-year-old son.

Dick and I had first become acquainted with the woman and her husband at a Christian Business Men's committee luncheon. We learned that their son was in the City of Hope with leukemia. From time to time when Dick was there, Tommy would wheel himself down the hall to visit him.

Today he was just returning after spending the weekend at home. He was pathetically thin, and his hair was sparse. The intravenous apparatus strapped to his arm was apparently his lifeline, for he was unable to take it off long enough to go from the car to his room.

"Hi, Tommy," I called. "Did you have a good Thanksgiving?"

"Yeah, it was nice. How's Dick?"

"Not too good. Tommy, this is our son, Bob."

After a hasty exchange of greetings, we quickly moved ahead of the pair. Bob shook his head, eyes flashing.

"That makes absolutely no sense! He's too young! There's no reason for that to happen!"

At first I was startled by the force of Bob's anger, then I began to see what was happening. Angry at God for allowing so much heartache and suffering to strike his father, Bob was projecting his intense feelings about Dick's illness onto Tommy. I knew it would take Bob time to work out his grief, just as it was taking me time. I still had flashes of anger about our battle with cancer.

There was a strange atmosphere in the room when we rejoined Dick—a kind of finality. Bob stood beside Dick's bed, holding his hand. He leaned over to hug Dick, and then he kissed him.

"Goodbye, Dad," Bob whispered.

"Goodbye, son."

They shook hands, and neither wanted to let go. The three of us wept together until it was time for Bob and me to walk silently back to the car. Bob flew home the next morning.

12

Released to Glory

"Do you know what they call this section of the hospital?" Dick asked several days later.

"No, do they have a special name for it?"

"It's Death Row. They bring you here to die. There's been one death today already."

I caught my breath and waited. The living grieve, and the dying sorrow, too.

"Dick, I brought the mail," I announced finally. "Here's a thick envelope from the realtor in Ohio."

Dick looked over the papers as he rested on the edge of the hospital bed. "The office is sold. All I need now is a Notary Public and the transaction will be complete."

I phoned a friend who is a Notary at the Narramore Foundation.

"Oh, Jeri, I was just on my way out the door to visit Dick!"

"Bring your notary stamp along, okay, Wally? We need you as a witness."

With that signature and the stamp, the last of Dick's preparations were complete. He leaned back in his bed and tried to relax. The nurses brought him pain medication more and more frequently. Dick dozed off and on, writhing and moaning, even as he slept. Occasionally I left the room to get away from his agony.

That night I waited outside Dick's room as a nurse made his bed. Leaning against the wall next to his door, I prayed. *Please, God, don't let me break down when we say goodnight.* I went back into his room.

The cold steel side rails were up, and I felt isolated from him. He looked like a little boy, tucked neatly between spotless white sheets. How I longed to gather his frail form into my arms, to hold him tightly. I had to ignore my impulse. The slightest touch would nearly have destroyed him.

"Is this your father?" a young nurse asked me.

"No . . . my husband," I whispered, hoping Dick hadn't heard. The expression on his face told me he had. He was only two years older than I, but the disease had aged him so much that he looked old enough to be my grandfather.

A shadow fell across the room, and I looked up. Dr. Wagner and his wife were silhouetted in the doorway. Mrs. Wagner stepped forward and stood next to me, while Dr. Wagner took Dick's hand.

"Hello, Dick." He stood quietly for a few minutes, praying.

I was overcome with gratitude. *Thank you, God. You knew I needed a friend, and you gave me the best I could have asked for. When Dr. Wagner said he'd stick by me, I had no idea it would be to this extent.*

A few minutes later, I leaned over Dick and whispered, "You mean everything to me, honey. I can't even tell you how much I appreciate everything you've done for me. Dick, I . . . " My voice broke.

Dick's eyes filled with tears as I kissed him gently on the forehead. Stepping quietly toward the door, I blew him a kiss. "I love you, Dick. Goodnight. I'll see you tomorrow."

Blindly finding my way to the parking lot, the tears I had held back for the past moments coursed down my face. My knees wobbly and my stomach tight with nausea, I stopped to lean against the building. *God! How much longer does this have to go on? Is this the end? Is this how Dick is going to die?"*

So many times before it had seemed the end. I had surrendered Dick, prepared for the worst, then he had rallied. He would come home for a few days or weeks or months, until the pain would grow intolerable. Then we would go back to the hospital again.

I must have faced Dick's death a thousand times. In my imagination, I had buried him over and over. This episode seemed much like the others. I had begun conditioning myself against thinking it was the last.

I managed to drive home somehow. The automatic garage door opened at the press of a button, and I gunned the motor to force my car up the steep driveway into its parking space. With another push of a button, the door rattled to a close behind me. Soon the garage light went off and I sat in the dark, too drained to move. Numb, I leaned over the steering wheel.

"God, what are you doing with our lives?" I wept bitterly. 'Where are you in all of this? I feel so alone."

Unsure that anyone was istening, I cried out to the Creator anyway. "Why? Why does it have to be this way? What is it you want from me? I want to keep going. I'm willing, but I . . . I just can't! You'll have to give me strength."

I don't know how long those moments of agony continued. Finally, gently, relief came.

Early the next morning the shrill ringing of the telephone startled me out of a deep sleep.

"Hello?"

"Jeri . . . Jeri, you've got to get the doctor. I can't . . . stand . . . the pain any . . . longer. It's just unbearable. Doc . . . he promised . . . "

"I'll call him right away, honey." I was wide awake, trembling. "I'll be there as soon as I can. I love you, Dick."

A sigh on the other end told me that everything was in my hands now. Frantically, I dialed the doctor.

"I'm on my way." The phone clicked abruptly in my ear.

I telephoned our pastor, then Dr. Wagner. We all agreed to meet at the hospital.

Speeding toward the City of Hope, my mind reeled faster than the car could move in the bustling early morning traffic. Unconsciously I turned at the right streets and entered the familiar grounds. Slamming the car door behind me, I flew in the direction of the hospital entrance.

Our pastor and his wife arrived at the door just as I did. We greeted each other somberly and walked together down the long hall to Dick's ward. Suddenly I heard Dick scream. I stopped in horror, then moved along mechanically. Dick's screaming grew louder as we approached. Framed by the open door, I watched him jerking, wrenching against his agony. My legs went limp, and I collapsed into the arms of our pastor's wife.

A nurse carefully injected intravenous pain medication into Dick's arm. The doctor had warned that this would be his last resort when the pain finally became uncontrollable. We all knew that it signaled the end.

For hours Dick's body alternately thrashed, grew quiet, then jerked violently again. His tortured cries often quieted to a mumble. Now and then he seemed to revert to his childhood, chuckling as if an unseen friend were conversing with him. Then came more wrenching, more groaning.

"Jesus must have felt like this . . . when he was dying," Dick whispered hoarsely to the pastor after one of his seizures.

Time ticked slowly away, and his cries lessened until he slipped into what appeared to be a deep sleep. His breathing became noticeably heavy and labored.

Our friend Tom came and sat with Dick for a long time, wiping tears away every now and then. Other friends came and went throughout the day, comforting me in my vigil. Bob and Lola May arrived late in the afternoon. They were an older couple whose parental love and support had strengthened me for months. Since Dick seemed to be peaceful at last, I decided to go home to get some rest.

As we stepped toward the exit, Lola May and I encountered two nurses.

"Would it be okay if I went home for some rest?" I asked hesitantly.

Their uncertain glances at each other told me something was different about *this* crisis, and that I should not go.

"I'll stay with you, Jeri," Lola May quckly offered.

Slowly, we returned to Dick's room, and Bob left. "He's not asleep, Mrs. Krumroy. He's in a coma," the nurse explained as I looked into Dick's ashen face.

"Should I find a private nurse for the night, then?"

She smiled kindly. "I'm your private nurse."

Thank you, God, I prayed, *for your thoughtful ways.*

Dick's heavy breathing became more labored as Lola May read aloud from the Psalms. The nurse, who we learned was a Christian, brought us some hot cinnamon rolls and cocoa. I had intended to pass the hours sitting by Dick's side, but the emotional strain was too exhausting. I simply had to rest.

"I'll stay with Dick, Jeri, and call you if there are any changes," Lola May whispered.

One of the nurses smiled as she gave me a pillow and a sheet. "The room next door is being remodeled, Mrs. Krumroy, but you can rest in there."

In the dark room I found a small couch among the furniture stacked in the middle and curled up to try to relax.

Lying there alone with my thoughts, I felt as though warm clouds were engulfing me. Never before had I been so totally surrounded by God's love.

When I awoke, the corridor was teeming with nurses and technicians hurrying in and out of the room across from Dick's. A Christian woman lay dying there, longing for the end to come quickly. I could hear her pleading, "Please, let me go."

Another door had been closed, a big taped sign announcing that the room was being sterilized for the next patient. Death was in the air.

Morning was approaching quickly, and I was still extremely tired. Could it be my imagination, or was Dick's breathing more labored? His room was dim, with occasional shadows caused by outside lights flashing against the walls. The nurse would tiptoe to Dick's bedside every five minutes and inject more pain medication into his I.V. Dick and I had determined to omit anything that would prolong his life when the time came. I felt comforted by that decision.

Glycerine-coated swabs had been left at his bedside by a thoughtful attendant. Gently, I began to apply the soothing ointment to his parched, swollen lips. My mind wandered to happier days. These were the lips that I had kissed that first wonderful time. They were the lips whispering countless loving words to me that had told me how beautiful I was. Dick's lips had spoken words of encouragement, assuring me that I *could* go on without him, but now would never again form the name "Jeri." These lips that I loved would be silent until that glorious day when he welcomes me into the presence of Jesus.

The room was taking on a strange odor now. I noticed Dick's hand opened and over his chest. As my eyes fell on his wedding band, the words we had repeated twenty-eight years before came to me. "With this ring I do wed . . . until death do us part." Gently, I lifted his finger and slipped off the ring. Never in the world had we expected that it would end this way.

Feeling helpless, I walked around the bed to toss the used swab into the wastebasket. Staring at Dick's shattered, shrunken body, I breathed a short, desperate prayer.

"Oh, God! Why don't you just take him?"

I had barely reached the other side of the bed, when a strange silence filled the room. The raspy, hard breathing had faded with his last sigh.

"Lola May," I stammered, "I think . . . I think Dick has gone to heaven.

Like a clock that had finally run down, Dick's body was still.

"That was the quickest answer to prayer I've ever seen," Lola May spoke softly.

"What prayer?"

"Yours. You asked God to take him, and he did."

How many times had I said that prayer before? At last, God had said yes.

"I'll get the nurse," Lola May offered.

She was gone only a few seconds, but in that time I saw clearly what appeared to be Dick's spirit flowing from his frail frame into the presence of Jesus. His spirit seemed to have the form of his body, but it appeared more like a vapor. I'm still unable to explain what took place in those sacred moments. The words of Jesus reassured me, "I am the resurrection and the life; he who believes in me shall live even if he dies, and everyone who lives and believes in me shall never die" (John 11:25, 26).

The nurse hurried into the room, followed by Lola May. After searching for his pulse, the nurse turned to me, paused, then spoke quietly. "Honey, he's with Jesus. God who's helped you through this trial will give you the strength to go on."

I didn't know how to react. Having plunged through the deep waters of grief and cried more bitter tears than could be counted, I felt a tremendous sense of release—I was almost lyrical with joy. *Gone to glory,* I wrote in my Bible. *Released from pain.*

Summers ago Dick and I had stood locked in each other's arms inside a little mountain cottage, praying that no matter what happened we would remember to cling to our favorite Bible promise. I'd had the words printed and framed for our twenty-fifth wedding anniversary.

We'd had no idea of the path before us, but God had engraved that verse upon our hearts. "For this God is our God for ever and ever: he will be our guide even unto death." Psalm 48:14 (KJV)

So it had been, through all the years before we said our final goodbye. God would keep his promise now, as I began to face the future on my own.

13

Climbing Up

The friendly crackle of a fire, the gentle creak of an old rocking chair, the soft murmurs of a sleeping newborn baby — these were the sounds that comforted me as I rocked my tiny grandson the day after Dick's funeral in Ohio. Snow fell quietly outside the window. I hadn't seen snow in years and had nearly forgotten how fragile and frosty a winter landscape can be. Chilly as it was outside, my memories of the past twenty-four hours were tender and warm.

I had kept my composure throughout the service. Only when the soloist sang "Through It All," our daughter's request, did I nearly break. Having endured so much, my heart swelled with gratitude that, through it all, God had been working in my heart. Dick was eulogized by several friends, and a tape was played in which Dr. Clyde Narramore spoke eloquently of Dick's life and faith.

> Surely those of us who worked shoulder to shoulder each day with Dick can never again be the same. We saw that through all of Dick's suffering God was gracious to him and saw him through. If this example had not been right before our eyes, we may never have been truly convicted and convinced of God's sustaining power through the valley of shadows of life . . .

As Dick's death and funeral faded quietly into the shadows too, the ever-flowing faucet of my tears was turned on and off for weeks. I seemed forever suspended between gratitude and grief. I was glad that Dick's pain was over, but I dreaded returning home. The day after Dick died, I had begun giving away his clothes. But there were more of his personal items, and I knew I needed to go through them. How could I give away his personal belongings? I couldn't bear the thought of destroying the past.

Dr. Wagner had warned me of the dangers of "over-memorializing." Shoes polished and ready in the closet, hairbrush on the dresser, setting a place for the unseen visitor, hanging a stocking for the deceased loved one at Christmas—all are signs of unwholesome grief, and I needed to avoid them.

No matter how much we loved each other, no matter how cherished the years we had together were, things would never again be the same. Memories are precious, but the world must go on. Memorializing Dick—surrounding myself with inner reminders and outward keepsakes—would keep healing from happening. I needed to put away old photos and other souvenirs, and get rid of items that would only prolong my sorrow.

I couldn't destroy the past—it had happened. I couldn't conquer grief. I could refuse to let it vanquish me, and I would choose not to feed it with Dick's personal belongings. Even so, I knnew it would be difficult.

There was another difficulty for which I wasn't prepared. For months after Dick's death I was plagued with repeated illness. Lingering colds, violent flu, sore throats—every germ seemed to set up residence in my body and wage war against my weakened resistance. At one point I broke out in a violent case of hives and ended up in the emergency room. The doctor said it was stress.

In reading books on grief, I discovered that illness often strikes a person who has been under great stress, and that the death of one's mate is a major cause of stress-related illness. I suspected that the bursitis in my arm had a lot to do with the injections I'd been forced to give Dick.

I further decided to go for a complete physical after I returned to California. While I waited for my appointment, the receptionist asked me to update their records for insurance purposes. Getting no further than the first line of the form, I stopped abruptly.

Miss or Mrs? Widowed, Single, or Divorced? Everything inside me rebelled. I didn't *want* to circle "widowed." I wasn't divorced. I didn't feel like a "Mrs." either, or for that matter, a "Miss." I could easily have checked a square labeled *misfit*.

Momentarily, I didn't know who I was or to whom I belonged. How could I fill out the rest of the form? I'd always belonged to a couples' world. I'd been known as Mrs. Richard Krumroy, wife of the successful builder, a title that had social status. Now I was single. My former life was shattered.

I sat in the office, reflecting on my earlier struggles and the lessons they had taught me. I remembered that Dr. Wagner had talked about three emotional feelings that contribute to our self-concept.

"They're like a three-legged stool, Jeri," he had explained as we sat in his office one morning. "If one leg is too short, the stool will wobble and totter. The three 'legs' are *belongingness, worthiness,* and *competence.*"

Belongingness means we feel a part of things. This was what I was struggling with now. It wasn't just having to put an "X" by the word "Widowed." It was a dreadful feeling of not *belonging* to anybody.

I'd first noticed it after I returned to California. During the final days of Dick's illness and just after, our friends from church had been highly visible. As the weeks went by, their phone calls came less frequently. It appeared as though they were avoiding me.

Why doesn't the phone ever ring? Why doesn't the pastor come, unless he's asked? I wondered sadly. *Everyone seems too busy to bother with me. How can those people be so insensitive to my needs now, when they flocked to the hospital the day Dick died.* I fumed, heartsick. *Don't they realize how lonely it is, driving home from church every Sunday to face an empty house?*

My feelings built into a grudge. Why couldn't they be more supportive? Soon I wanted nothing to do with that church. Even hearing its name brought my negative feelings to the surface. It was a long time before my anger was released. I came to realize that people couldn't have done much to help me through my grief process, but they could have allowed me to know they cared and were still praying for me. Acknowledging a person's grief and being a friend is much more important than saying the right words.

Through the years since Dick's death, I've learned that sensitivity can be expressed in simple ways. "I'm so sorry," "You've been on my mind for the past few days," or "I'll stick by you the best I can," can work wonders with a grieving heart. What we need most is to know that someone genuinely cares about us and understands our grief.

No one has a magic formula for caring. Words in themselves can be empty, even hurtful. Some things shouldn't be said. "He's going to be all right," spoken to the spouse of a terminally ill patient, is unwise, for we cannot predict the future. Christians seem to fall victim to countless other platitudes. "God has a purpose in all this" and "All things work together for good" are true biblical statements. Nevertheless, they sound hollow to suffering ears.

How often do we hear, "Well, she's with the Lord." "He's out of his misery." "God will supply your needs." What people are really saying is, "These phrases should snap you out of your grief. So why don't you snap?" We hate to frustrate our comforter, but we don't feel a bit better for all her sage words.

Not all words are wise. Sometimes people say things that are just plain tactless or stupid. At Dick's funeral a woman turned to me and said, "So. When do you think you'll be getting married again?" Her lack of sensitivity was nothing compared to the cruelty of some other people.

A friend of mine who lost her little boy was suffering bravely, though her heart was broken. She received a note one day that read, "You're probably rejoicing now because you know that your son is in heaven. And, after all, you have three others!" Rejoicing? "I didn't feel like rejoicing at all," she recalled bitterly.

The kindest thing a friend can do is to put concern into action. Weeping with someone, without the usual cliches, can be far more helpful and encouraging than reciting endless Bible verses. No matter how true the words of the

Bible are, grief can momentarily close our ears to them.

Loving, being there, and providing a strong shoulder is worth a thousand words or a hundred thousand platitudes. A well-spoken prayer, offered in the presence of the sorrowing friend, may be all that is needed.

Sensitivity to the hurts of others can be expressed quietly behind the scenes, too. Asking friends to pray, suggesting that they send cards or flowers, or arranging for them to visit at an appropriate time is a worthwhile way to reach out.

Caring for the bereaved has no time limit. I had time to work through much of my grief before Dick and I said goodbye. Many others must face this climb from the pit of despair afterward. For some, the pit is deeper and darker. Saying, "I think you've grieved long enough. It's time you snapped out of this" only makes the upward climb harder.

No one can know how long is "long enough." It depends on the maturity of the person. That decision is not up to us. The best thing we can do is to encourage a grieving person to talk through their pain. Professional counsel often can uncover emotions that prolong the grieving process unnecessarily.

By putting ourselves into the shoes of others, we can begin to understand the emotional distress that frequently accompanies grief. Even if we have never lost a loved one, we can imagine what it must be like to feel unworthy of friendships, to feel we don't belong, to feel incompetent in facing life alone. By understanding with a heart of love, we can reach out with compassion that can be felt. It is through this feeling that healing comes.

I had the feeling also that people felt awkward about reaching out to me. They were not comfortable about mentioning Dick's name, even though I wanted very much to talk about him. I wanted to tell funny stories about him and to share those last moments of his life with other people. Yet those others were uneasy unless I controlled my feelings by holding back my grief and my tears. I felt isolated, pushed into a corner.

One day I stood at the church door, talking to a male member of the congregation. Suddenly his wife rushed up to him and grabbed his arm. She threw me a glance that clearly said, "Hands off! He's mine!"

I had heard that some women, especially if they are insecure, feel threatened by the presence of a widow or a divorced woman. I had never thought of myself as a threat, and I was wounded when I was treated that way.

Sunday after Sunday I drove home in tears, feeling alone and rejected. I needed the friendship of others so desperately that I finally decided to find a church where I could feel more comfortable. I called my pastor and told him why I was leaving. He voiced little understanding of my feelings. Instead, he placed the responsibility for my loneliness in my own lap.

"You have to be a friend to have friends, Jeri," he chided. "Reach out!"

I had no energy to reach out, to take risks. My grief had rendered me helpless, and I desperately needed someone to recognize that. Since then I have talked with many grieving people, and was somewhat surprised to discover that a feeling of isolation is a common theme among them.

"At my wife's funeral I was asked to have a meal with so many people, I wondered if I would ever have time to fit them all into my schedule," one man told me. "In nine months, only one couple ever followed through." He was shocked and disappointed—wounded further by those who had seemed so willing to offer comfort.

Grief is a solitary experience, in a way, and only those who have experienced it can really know how to comfort one another. I resolved never to allow my sorrow to be wasted—I would reach out to those who hurt whenever I could.

Today I can envision several ways in which churches can improve their frequently poor performance in this area. Perhaps the church could publish a monthly listing of the needs of widows and widowers. A committee could be established to aid the bereaved, providing practical as well as emotional support. Some churches have organized informal "Adopt-A-Widow" programs in which couples assume the responsibility of shopping, gardening, cooking, or cleaning for bereaved members.

Having lost my own husband, I can understand the vulnerability of widows and widowers and our need for loving counsel. The church can provide comfort in this area, too. When we feel the pangs of having lost our dearest love, we long to feel special again.

Unfortunately, in many congregations the social structure is geared to couples. In this setting, we may find ourselves competing with wives or husbands.

The situation is aggravated when we enjoy the company of one man or one woman in particular. It is difficult for us to simply like a member of the opposite sex without wanting an extra measure of their attention. That doesn't necessarily mean we're interested in romance. Often we only want the kind of personal verification that we once received from our spouses. This social tension adds to our vulnerability. Sometimes our married friends reject us because they fear that we are going to lure their mates away.

We face an altogether different set of difficulties in the company of other singles. Rushing into marriage can open a Pandora's box of problems, including failed marriages or other emotional disorders. Loneliness often opens us to shallow romances. When physical affection which we may not have enjoyed for some time is expressed, emotional blinders go on, and reality may slip out the side door. All too late the remaining spouse may discover that they have made an unfortunate mistake. Creating a climate of love and understanding is the most gracious gift a church can bestow upon a grieving member.

Widowed people are especially vulnerable to sorrow and loneliness during holidays. Isolation is more threatening and loneliness more painful on a day that was once shared with a departed loved one. Reaching out at such a time pays great dividends. Surely the church can ease the emptiness of those who have no families to care about them. Surely the joy on a lonely person's face will make the family Christmas lights shine a little brighter, or cause the birthday candles to glow more warmly than ever. All these ways of expressing love can assure bereaved people that they still *belong*.

Belongingness was not the only emotion that was under attack in my life. My sense of *worthiness* also was being challenged. One night I was invited to a combination anniversary and birthday party. Sitting alone among four couples in the festively decorated dining room, I grew more and more depressed.

God, why did you allow them to be married forty years when I only had twenty-eight? What did I do wrong? Didn't I deserve more? My thoughts haunted me. Tears stung my eyes from time to time, and my friends' laughter sounded far away and hollow.

At home alone, I thought about these emotions. Why should I feel envious? I was thankful for the wonderful memories of the twenty-eight years that God had given us. Dick was gone, but I was alive, Life ahead could be empty or meaningful—it was up to me. God still had a purpose for my life. I should not feel guilty for living, for enjoying, for sharing.

Yet it was difficult. Such resolve seemed to me to be a lot like lifting myself up by my own bootstraps. God communicates love and forgiveness best through the warm bodies, open hearts, and loving spirits of people; through tender hands, willing feet, tamed tongues, and caring communities.

I'm reminded of the story of five-year-old Shelly who expressed this inward need of all of us one night.

"I'm scared, mommy."

"Go to sleep, Shelly. Everything's okay."

I can't sleep. I'm scared of the dark. I keep imagining all kinds of things.

With a sigh, her mother crawled out of bed, turned on the hall light, and sat on the edge of Shelly's bed.

"Everything's all right, honey. God is watching over you. You don't have to be afraid."

"I know, mommy, but I want somebody with skin on.

Sometimes the darkness of our emotional world needs "somebody with skin on" to brighten the way. God provided this for me one weekend. I went on a spiritual retreat with some people I'd met after Dick's death. We did a lot of sharing and discussing.

Leaving the room later, I cornered one of the pastors. "Did I talk a lot about myself and my husband?"

He seemed reluctant to answer.

"Be honest with me," I urged.

"Yes," he admitted, his eyes serious. "I guess you did,"

"Well, how did you react to that? Did it bother you?"

His answer was a turning point for me.

"Jeri," he smiled, his face reflecting kindness, "we love and accept you for *you* not for somebody we didn't know." From that moment, I began to see myself as a valuable person.

14
Learning to Stand

I must have doubted my own competence a thousand times in the years surrounding Dick's illness. When that doubt eased, fear and anxiety took over. It was difficult to trust my own ability to make decisions.

In the months that followed the funeral, it was even more of a struggle. Finally, one day, I knew it was time to force myself to make a decision. I went into the dining room, opened my china cabinet and saw that new dishes were definitely in order. I grabbed my purse and headed for the shopping mall.

Looking at china, I found myself thinking, *Now, what would Dick like? No, it doesn't matter now. This is* my *decision,* my *preference.* Even so, I tried to get the clerk to decide for me. Finally I purchased a dinner plate from each of three different sets and took them home.

When one of my neighbors dropped in for a visit, I showed her the plates. "Which one do you like best?" I asked.

When she pointed to the design I favored, my decision was made. I returned the other two plates and ordered service for twelve in my new pattern. It was fun to take the odds and ends out of the cupboard and put the new china in. It was time to have company.

I cried as I set the table for seven one evening. It was too much for me to be the odd person alone. My grief turned to self-pity. The dependent person waits for someone else to do the planning. I soon discovered that if my life were going to be interesting, I would have to make my own plans. Otherwise, I'd end up sitting at home.

I felt like a wobbly colt learning to stand alone. I struggled with the loneliness of entering an empty house, hating the silence. I turned on the television or radio and kept it on most of the time. I was lost in our king-sized bed, and many nights I ended up hugging Dick's pillow. Night after night I cried myself to sleep.

One Saturday afternoon I couldn't stand myself any more. Gathering up my coat and purse, I drove to a movie theater. I bought the biggest bag of popcorn with the largest soft drink sold, and I sat through the double feature alone. When I emerged from the theater I was surprised to realize I'd actually enjoyed myself. I was capable of making my own plans and enjoying them.

A widow once told me, "I'm afraid to eat in a restaurant alone. What would people think? I won't even go to church alone." It *is* hard, when you're used to having a companion, to sit alone in a coffee shop. I know, because I had my own struggle. Reluctantly I would get dressed up, buy a newspaper, enter a restaurant, and courageously order breakfast for one. I could always hide behind the classified ads, I reasoned.

One morning I noticed another single woman waiting to be seated. I motioned to my waitress. "Tell her she can eat with me," I suggested.

"Oh, thank you," the woman beamed. "I need some company today."

"My name's Jeri Krumroy," I smiled as we shook hands.

"Leah. Leah Ford."

"Coffee?" the waitress asked, poised above an empty cup.

"Thank you. Yes."

"Do you come here often?" I asked, trying to make conversation.

"No. I hate being alone, so I don't go out much . . . "

I soon discovered that she was a Christian, and we had a marvelous time getting acquainted.

I could have allowed my fear of being alone to hold me captive and keep me from happy relationships. I was determined not to let anxiety block my self-confidence. As I asserted myself, God began to bolster my faltering self-esteem. An awareness of my place in Christ helped. Having trusted in him, Jesus made me part of his family. The Bible says "As many as received Him, to them He gave the right to become children of God, even to those who believe in His name" (John 1:12).

My responsibility is to place my life in God's hands, to release myself from self-condemnation. *No* one has the right to make me feel guilty.

> Who will bring a charge against God's elect? God is the One who justifies; who is the one who condemns? Christ Jesus is He who died, yes, rather who was raised, who is at the right hand of God, who also intercedes for us.
>
> Romans 8:33, 34

My sense of self-esteem is rooted in the Holy Spirit who has chosen to live in and work through me. I know that I belong because I am a member of God's family. I know that I am worthy because the blood of Jesus cleanses me from all sin. I know that I am competent because God's Spirit is enabling me, encouraging me, and empowering me. Looking back, I can see the ways in which God worked in my life.

I felt incapable of getting a job. What kind would I get? Who would want me? I'd never find work . . . but I did.

It seemed physically impossible for me to give Dick his pain injections . . . but I did.

I believed I couldn't face his funeral . . . but I did.

I was afraid to stay at home alone nights . . . but I did.

I could not imagine myself walking into a restaurant by myself, with only a newspaper for company . . . but I did.

I could not picture myself a single woman mingling with couples at social events . . . but I do.

Because I was willing to become my own person, and to face life with confidence, I discovered the wonderful phrase, "I can!"

With God's all-powerful help, I can enjoy relationships, accept responsibilities, and face the future alone. I have learned to cope, to take the initiative, to assert myself when necessary.

Through the gentle teaching of God and insights from professional counseling, I learned to deal with my emotions and emerge like a beautiful butterfly, a whole person.

15

Finding Myself

In the months and years that followed Dick's death, I discovered several ways to handle my grief. I continued my sessions with Dr. Wagner because I knew that supressing my feelings would only cause them to erupt psychologically or physically in the long run. At the same time, I realized how important it was to separate myself from Dick and from his influences on my life.

One way to do that was to redecorate our—my—home. I thought about it for some time, but always ended up asking myself "why?" After all, who cared? Some days I didn't even make my bed. Eventually I came to the realization that *I* am an important person. I could do things for me, just for me, and enjoy them. I arranged to have the house painted inside and out, bought new drapes and carpeting, and put new wallpaper in the bathroom. I also went on a diet and changed my hairstyle. These changes gave me a sense of decisiveness. They fostered more positive feelings such as being in control of my choices.

Another way in which I came to terms with my grief was in accepting my life without Dick. That readjustment was all the more difficult when I thought about facing problems Dick had always handled in the past. "What if I have plumbing problems?" I asked myself. "What if the car breaks down?" My anxiety about potential problems was compounded by my resentment. In a sense, I felt abandoned. My grief was more for myself than it was for Dick.

One summer morning my feeling of abandonment confronted me head-on. When the alarm rang I rolled over in bed to turn it off. I sat up and stretched, then stepped out of bed. As I slipped on my robe and slippers, a strange sound hummed in the back of my head. I wandered out to the kitchen to fix my morning coffee, and the sound grew louder, more insistent.

Suddenly my feet felt wet. The carpet in the entryway and the dining room was under water! "Oh no!" I cried. I sloshed into the kitchen and opened the cupboard under the kitchen sink. A pipe had burst, and water gushed everywhere.

"Oh, God! What should I do?" I hurried to the phone and called my neighbor.

"Mary, a pipe burst in my kitchen and there's water all over the place!"

"Don't worry, Jeri," she said. "Roy will be right over."

A few minutes later Roy ran over, still dressed in his pajamas. He was carrying a wrench. He hurried into the kitchen and managed to turn the water off.

"That will take care of it until you can get a plumber, Jeri," he said. "See you later!" With that, he was gone.

"That's all?" I said to the empty room. "See you later? God, what am I going to do?" I ran back into my bedroom, threw myself on the bed and cried. "Why have you abandoned me like this, Lord?" I wept.

Jeri, now is no time for a pity party. Just get the Yellow Pages.

I sat up and wiped my tears, then found the telephone book. First I called a plumber, then found a nearby carpet cleaner who said he could take care of the mess. Within a matter of minutes, the carpet crew arrived and started mopping up. The plumber came several hours later making quick work of the repairs.

In the meantime, neighborhood teenagers arrived, beach towels in hand, to enjoy my swimming pool. My "open door" policy about the pool had given me hours of pleasure with the neighborhood kids, but this time I thought, *why today?*

While the workers were cleaning up the water, I went out to the pool. I had recently purchased some deck chairs, and I wandered over to sit in one. Suddenly the chair gave way beneath me, and I hit the cement, hard. The force of the fall knocked the wind out of me for a few seconds, and the pain in my back was excruciating.

"Mrs. Krumroy!" one of the boys shouted as he ran to me. "Are you all right?" I whispered. "Don't touch me. Just let me sit here a minute while I catch my breath." After a few minutes, convinced that my tailbone was broken, I was able to get up, but the pain was awful. I urged the kids to go on with their swimming, and made my way back into the house.

"Hey, lady," one of the men said, "we're going to have to take this carpet up and stretch it to dry. I can't guarantee it will look very good when we re-lay it."

"Do you think I should replace it?" I asked.

"It's your decision, lady."

My decision. *My* decision. Every day God seemed to be putting me into situations that forced me to make decisions alone. *Who will help me on this one? What should I do?*

"Could I put new linoleum in here?" I asked.

"Sure. You can do whatever you want."

I can, can't I? I can do whatever I want! "Do you sell linoleum?"

"Yeah. But whatever you decide, lady, we can't do anything more until you empty that hutch, there, and move it outside." He nodded in the direction of my china cabinet.

My tailbone was hurting so badly that I could hardly think. I knew I could never empty that cabinet on my own —let alone *move* the thing. I eased my way out to the pool.

"Okay, guys!" I shouted at the kids. "I'm calling in my debts. I need your help!"

Eagerly the kids climbed out of the water, toweled off, and followed me into the dining room. I found some boxes in the garage. They carefully unloaded the china cabinet, placing the boxes in the living room. Then several of the boys worked together to move the cabinet out of the sliding glass door that led from the dining room to the side of the house.

"Can you take me to your store to select some flooring?" I asked one of the men.

"Sure, lady. But all this old stuff will have to come out.

We can do it this afternoon."

By afternoon I'd selected new flooring, *all by myself* with no one's opinion but my own. The men had dragged out the old carpeting. When it was dry, they would cut it to fit my two bathrooms. There was only one problem.

"What about this mess?" I asked the fellow in charge as I pointed to several large piles of old lineoleum. "Aren't you going to clean it up?"

"Sorry, lady. That's your responsibility."

"I only have two trash barrels. This would fill at least a dozen!"

"Sorry. We'll be back tomorrow to lay the carpet in the bathroom. It should be dry by then." With that, he and his men climbed into their truck and took off.

"Look at this mess!" I groaned. "What am I going to do about this?" I limped out to the back yard, past the now-quiet pool and through the gate to the Narramore Foundation property. Just then one of the groundskeepers drove toward me on a little tractor.

"Hi, Jeri! How's it going?" he called as he pulled up beside me and stopped the motor.

I shook my head. "You'd never believe the day I've had!" I told him everything, and finished with a sigh. "Now I'm stuck with a half-dozen piles of used linoleum. It looks like the walls of Jerico in there!''

"Aw, that's no problem. I'll swing around in one of the trucks and pick it up. We can dump it in one of our big trash dumpsters. I'll be around in a few minutes."

That night I stood in my kitchen, looking at my new floor. "Holy Spirit," I prayed, "you really did walk beside me today. You gave me wisdom and guidance and comfort, and I was able to make my *own* decisions. Thank you!"

The Bible tells us through the prophet Isaiah that God is the husband of the widowed:

> Fear not; for thou shalt not be ashamed: neither
> be thou confounded; for thou shalt not be put to
> shame: for thou shalt forget the shame of thy youth,

and shalt not remember the reproach of thy widow-
hood anymore. For thy Maker is thine husband; the
Lord of hosts is his name; and thy Redeemer the Holy
One of Israel; the God of the whole earth shall he be
called. For the Lord hath called thee as a woman for-
saken and grieved in spirit, and a wife of youth, when
thou wast refused, saith thy God.

Isaiah 54:46 (KJV)

God *had* been with me that day. He had cared for me,
protected me, provided for me, and he had encouraged me
to grow by giving me confidence in my own choices. I
slipped into bed at night exhausted and aching, but my self-
confidence and my self-esteem were at a new high.

Several months later I walked into the kitchen one
afternoon and was startled by a rustling sound in the bottom cupboard near my refrigerator. As I stood listening, the
rustling grew louder, and suddenly a sick feeling hit me in
the stomach.

"Oh, no! Please say it isn't true!" I said out loud, I
walked over to the cupboard and lightly tapped on the
door. The rustling stopped. I closed my eyes and buried my
face in my hand.

Well, there's only one thing to do, I told myself. I
picked up my purse and my keys and headed out to the car.
At the hardware store I purchased a small mouse trap, then
stopped at the grocery store for some cheese.

Back home I carefully set the trap and put it in the
cupboard. "Please, God, don't let this be messy!" I begged.

The next morning I opened the cupboard. The prayer
was answered in a sense. It wasn't messy at all. The mouse
had neatly stolen the cheese, and the trap stood poised,
still ready to catch my tiny intruder.

At work that morning I asked several people how to
catch a mouse. I was surprised by the variety of recipes for
mouse bait, but finally settled on one. I took a ball of
cheese and covered it with peanut butter, then wrapped a
piece of bacon around it. I tied a piece of thread around
the morsel and put it on a larger mouse trap.

"Here you go, little fellow," I said. "A gift-wrapped submarine sandwich, just for you."

Later that night I heard the rustling again, then a loud snap. Suddenly my kitchen was alive with the racket. *That mouse must be huge!* I told myself. On and on the noise continued. I ran out into the yard.

"Please, Lord," I prayed, "let the mouse die with dignity. And please, please, don't let it be too messy!"

I waited for about fifteen minutes, then walked back into the kitchen. It was quiet. I stood by the cupboard for several minutes, took a deep breath and opened the door. There he was—the tiniest mouse I had ever seen, looking up at me with soulful eyes. He wasn't dead at all. He was caught by the tail!

I picked up the trap and took it outside. "Okay, little fellow," I said. "Looks like you've been reprieved. Now you go visit someone else's kitchen, and don't come back to mine!" I released the spring on the trap and the mouse ran away. I shook my head and wandered back into the kitchen.

As I took everything out of the cupboard, washed it and replaced the shelf paper, I smiled to myself. Another crisis handled, and this time I hadn't reacted with anger or resentment or fear. I'd asked for advice, but I'd made my own decisions.

It felt great to be on the road to recovery. My mood swings occurred less frequently, and I assumed more responsibility for my own feelings and decisions. Even my sense of humor had returned. I knew that I could not escape from grief, but I came to realize that enduring bereavement without resentment is a worthy goal.

The unique aspect of Christian grief is that while our mates can leave us, God never does. In Romans 8:35–39 Paul tells us that nothing can separate us from God's care and love:

Who shall separate us from the love of Christ? shall tribulation, or distress, or persecution, or famine, or nakedness, or peril, or sword? As it is written, For thy sake we are killed all the day long; we are accounted as sheep for the slaughter. Nay, in all these things we are more than conquerors through him that loved us. For I am persuaded, that neither death, nor life, nor angels, nor principalities, nor powers, nor things present, nor things to come, nor height, nor depth, nor any other creature, shall be able to separate us from the love of God, which is in Christ Jesus our Lord. (KJV)

As Christians we have a vital relationship with God—a relationship which gives meaning and purpose to life, in spite of our grief. Because of that, we can look to the future with hope, seeing life as a challenge and not as a threat. The prophet Jeremiah said it this way: "For I know the plans that I have for you," declares the Lord, "plans for welfare and not for calamity to give you a future and a hope" (Jeremiah 29:11).

God's plans for me include helping me to learn to make plans for myself. As a dependent person, I'd developed the habit of letting others decide for me what I would do with my time. Again and again I found myself alone because I failed to make plans for myself. This was especially true of the weekends.

Finally I decided to make arrangements for some weekend activity. I called a single friend and asked her if she would like to spend the weekend with me. She readily accepted.

"Let's go over to the golf course and play a few holes," she said on Saturday morning as we were finishing breakfast.

"I've never swung at a ball in my life!" I responded.

"Nothing to it," Louise said. "Come on—you'll enjoy it."

"Let's go." I answered.

We drove out to the public golf course, and I discovered a whole new world. What fun to see the ball sailing down the fairway toward the green! The air was fresh and invigorating.

When we finished our game, I wandered into the pro shop and purchased a pair of golf shoes that were on sale — half price! Then I signed up for lessons.

In the weeks that followed, I discovered many advantages to playing golf. Hitting the ball was an excellent way to work out my frustrations, and walking helped relieve stress and anxiety. Golf was also a wonderful remedy for loneliness. A single person can go alone, and ask to be teamed with a threesome or foursome.

One day I was teamed with three men who were obviously oldtimers at the game. The fact that I was a novice soon became apparent to all of us, and finally I said, "Oh, I am sorry for holding you up. Why don't you three play, and I'll just tag along and study your technique."

"Not at all, Mrs. Krumroy," one of the men said. "You'll only get better with practice."

I was grateful for his graciousness, and although I'll never be a pro, eventually I learned to hold my own on the golf course. On the days when I was able to play with a friend, we had brunch following our game.

I continued my membership at the health spa, where I made new friends with interesting women. Together we shared our experiences, and some of them joined me in home Bible studies or went with me to plays or on outings.

The more I shared myself with others, the more healing took place in my life. I thought I was almost over my pain when one autumn day, my office phone rang. A woman asked me if I would speak at her woman's group in a few weeks. She wanted me to talk about grief.

"Yes," I said. "I'll be happy to do that. What day?"

"December 14."

I felt a vague uneasiness. "Hmm," I said. "There's nothing on my calendar, but I have a feeling I'm supposed to do something that day. Let me check my other calendar and I'll get back to you."

Later that day I looked at my calendar at home, but it was blank. I called the woman and confirmed our date.

Thanksgiving came and went, and a few days before I was scheduled to speak, I realized with horror why I had felt so uneasy about the date of the grief seminar. It was the second anniversary of Dick's death.

How could I possibly go through with it? I hurried to my telephone book to call the woman, but something stopped me. As I stood in front of the telephone, I recalled the moment several years ago when I had stood alone and heartbroken under the silent stars in my backyard.

I had been angry, then. At God. At the world. At disease. At Dick. Yet beneath my hurt, I sensed that God was preparing me for something. In my turmoil, I had reached a turning point. Then I began to bargain.

"God," I had said, "if you will give me back the peace and joy of my salvation, I'll share my experiences with others."

I was being taken at my word. From that moment, a greater love for the wounded began to grow in my heart. As Dick's condition worsened and as my own pain grew, I wondered what I would say to people who hurt. What possible good would come from my sorrow? Out of the furnace of my suffering, God has poured a metal of sensitivity and understanding that I could not have imagined then.

The apostle Paul explained the fruit of sorrow in this way:

> Blessed be the God and Father of our Lord Jesus Christ, the Father of mercies and God of all comfort; who comforts us in all our affliction so that we may be able to comfort others with the comfort with which we ourselves are comforted by God.
>
> For just as the sufferings of Christ are ours in abundance, so also our comfort is abundant through Christ.
>
> But if we are afflicted, it is for your comfort and salvation; or if we are comforted, it is for your comfort, which is effective in patient enduring of the same sufferings which we also suffer; and our hope for you is firmly grounded, knowing that as you are sharers of

our sufferings, so also you are sharers of our comfort.
2 Corinthians 1:37

Instead of cancelling an opportunity to share, I made myself go. I dressed in bright colors and was extra careful with makeup.

"One of life's wilderness experiences comes when we lose someone we love in death," I began. "No matter how at ease we feel in other situations, we often feel unsure of what to say or how to act in the presence of grief. Death is certain. No one escapes."

Suddenly my throat tightened, and I felt my eyes burning. I swallowed. "Grief is a process," I continued, "but it is not forever. It takes time to heal from the anguish, and it takes tangible people to help bridge the gap between the grieving person and God. Grief hurts—deeply—and sometimes there is little one can say or do to soften the blow."

Suddenly I was overcome, and I broke down. I stood weeping before the roomful of bewildered people, fighting to regain my composure. Finally I was able to explain.

"I am sorry," I said as I wiped my eyes with a tissue. "As I said earlier, grief is a process. It takes time, and sometimes our scars hurt us. This is the second anniversary of my husband's death, and I'd like to share with you how God provided for me throughout the ordeal."

That evening, three women committed their lives to a personal relationship with God through Christ. In the redemption of those women, God began redeeming my pain. In the years since then, I've shared my story in many more seminars and in private counseling sessions, and God has allowed me to help others who hurt.

Helping the bereaved is not easy. Vulnerability is the high price we pay for caring. Often when I share my story, the wound of my loss is painfully reopened because, although God is in the business of healing broken hearts, a scar always remains. Bereavement changes our lives forever.

16
Still Single?

After five years of being single, it became embarrassing when countless friends kept asking, "Are you still single? Why haven't you remarried?"

I wondered, too. I'd loved being married, a homemaker, and a mother. The single life is not one I would ever have chosen for myself. Why, I wondered, hadn't God brought another wonderful man into my life? Where was "Mr. Right"?

I dated again. Well-intentioned friends introduced me to eligible men.

"He's a fine Christian," I was told one time.

I looked forward to dinner with this new friend. I'd been so used to opening the door for Dick that I automatically opened it for Mike. We laughed and I felt good about his sense of humor. Over dinner, our conversation turned to God.

"I always went to church with my wife, Jeri," Mike said. "Of course, she was the religious one in the family. I guess, after all, religion is a woman's thing."

My heart sank. "But Mike," I said, "Christianity isn't just a 'religion' or doctrine—it's a personal relationship with God. We all need to know God as individuals."

"Oh, I believe in God," Mike answered. "I just don't believe in getting carried away, that's all."

It was raining that evening and I wore fashionable rain boots to go with my suit. Arriving home Mike offered to help me take them off. I said, "Oh, I can do that." He gently pushed me down in a chair and said, "Lady, can't you let anyone do something for you!" Was I becoming too independent? There had to be a balance.

When Mike called the next night, I said, "I'm really sorry, but I don't think I'm God's choice for you. Our priorities are different." I felt so alone. *Perhaps I could go on dating him for awhile,* I said to myself. *Maybe I could lead him to Christ.*

But the thought had barely run its course before I knew it wasn't right. If I continued to date Mike, we might fall in love. Scripture is clear on the issue of marrying an unbeliever: "Do not be bound together with unbelievers; for what partnership have righteousness and lawlessness . . . what has a believer in common with an unbeliever (2 Corinthians 6:14–15)?"

Tearfully, I talked with God. "I'm angry about this, Lord," I said. "I don't understand why you won't help me find a husband. I want so much to be married again. But more than that, I want to be what and where you want me."

Gently I felt the peace and comfort of God's love spread over me. It was as though a parent had wrapped their arms around me and rocked me tenderly, soothing my wounded, lonely self.

I continued my work as Coordinator for the Discovery Day programs, and this gave me opportunity to meet many new friends. They would come for a weekend or for a week, and we would share with each other. Sometimes I had people stay in my home. But it was always painful to watch them get in their cars and drive away. It seemed as though I was going through a series of mini-bereavements. Although I maintained friendships with many friends through letter writing, still, it was difficult to see them leave.

One day I decided that I couldn't stand to say goodbye one more time, and for the next few weeks I withdrew from people. If I were not friendly, perhaps I wouldn't feel their loss so much. Without human relationships, however, our lives are filled with despair, and once again I decided to risk myself.

One gentleman came to a grief seminar at the Foundation, and I liked him right away. He was gracious and gentle, and it felt good to be on the receiving end of his attentiveness. We went out to dinner several times, and then one night he said, "Jeri, I care deeply for you. You are so special. Would you consider marrying me?"

I took his hand. "Ted," I said, "It's too soon for you. You lost your wife less than a year ago. You need more time for your grief. You don't love me—not yet. Give yourself at least another year before you think about another marriage.

He shook his head sadly. "I can't do that, Jeri. I need a wife."

Four months later I heard that Ted had married, and within another year, he was divorced. Remarriage is not the solution to grief. I knew that. Still, I understood the cry of Ted's heart. I wanted to be married, too. Because Dick had leaned on me for so long, I sometimes had felt like his crutch. It felt good to walk with a healthy man with strong arms again.

Although I tried to be careful about dating, it wasn't always easy to discern what the men would be like. One evening I had a delightful time with a Christian man. We stopped for coffee on the way home from a play.

"Jeri, tomorrow's Saturday, and neither of us has to go to work. How about coming down to the beach with me for the night? I'm housesitting for a friend."

"I'm afraid I couldn't do that," I said sadly. "I'm a Christian."

"So am I," he said.

"But I could never live with my conscience," I said, "if I disobeyed God's standards for living. I don't drink and I don't smoke and I don't go to bed with men. I think you'd better take me home."

It was hard to do that. Vulnerability runs high in the first years of aloneness. Sexual feelings are strong. Yet I believe God's desire is clear:

> I urge you therefore, brethren, by the mercies of God, to present your bodies a living and holy sacrifice, acceptable to God, which is your spiritual service of worship. And do not be conformed to this world, but be transformed by the renewing of your mind, that you

may prove what the will of God is, that which is good
and acceptable and perfect.

Romans 12:-2

As the months went by, I went on singles' cruises and
to retreats, and I met many men. Each time I dated, I felt as
though I was on a mission field.

"What's wrong with me, God? Why can't I attract a
man who shares my values with maturity in Christ?"

Off and on during the six years following Dick's death,
I dated one man who made me feel special. Jim was strong
and yet gentle, and I enjoyed his company. We could relax
and be ourselves together. As the months went by, it felt
right to be with him. A widower, he attended some seminars
at the Narramore Christian Foundation and took some of
the psychological tests. He seemed to share my Christian
values and beliefs.

We saw more and more of each other until it seemed
natural to plan to spend my free time with him. He treated
me like a queen, and he never asked me to compromise my
values. Little by little I allowed myself to think that this
might be God's choice for me.

One moonlit autumn night, Jim asked me the question
I'd been praying for.

"I love you, Jeri. Will you marry me?"

"Oh, yes, Jim. I will!"

The crisis years with Dick had taught me one thing.
Nothing can replace the value of good counseling, and yet
most of us wait to get counseling until we're hurting. I've
begun to realize that all of us can benefit from 'preventive'
counseling, much the way we benefit from regular dental
and physical checkups.

Premarital counseling can detect problem areas
before they develop into real problems. It can show
couples how to communicate their love more effectively,
and provide the tools for mutual growth and satisfaction.
Because I felt so strongly about it, Jim agreed to take time

for premarital counseling at the Foundation.

We set the date for a spring wedding and planned our reception and honeymoon. Thanksgiving was spent with friends in Phoenix, and I shopped for my trousseau. By the first of the year I had selected a beautiful dress and a lovely hat for my wedding day. I ordered two hundred invitations.

Meanwhile, I gave my notice to the Narramore Christian Foundation. It would seem strange, not going to work every day, but I wanted to make a home for my new husband. I didn't want to balance a career with a new marriage.

Every weekend Jim and I shopped for a new home. From our counseling, we discovered that it would be best for us to start fresh, in a home that held no memories of Dick or of Jim's first wife. Finally we found exactly what we wanted, and started escrow proceedings. I was thrilled that God was giving me the desire of my heart.

At home I gathered boxes and placed them in every room of my little house. Somehow, I couldn't get started on filling them. Each day as I came in from work, I saw the stack of wedding invitations. Whenever I began to address them, I felt distracted. The time to mail them was coming closer as the date for our wedding drew near, the peace I felt one week became doubt the next.

"What is wrong, God?" I prayed one morning. Our wedding day was just four weeks away. "You've said in your Word that you are not the author of confusion, but of peace. Yet I am confused and troubled. I want Jim, but I also want your will for my life. Please, show me clearly today what I need to know."

Actually, a problem involving our families *had* surfaced during premarriage counseling which we had been unable to work out. It was important enough that, unsolved, it would have had serious consequences for our marriage. Jim usually called me every evening, but this evening I had a reception at the Foundation to attend, so I called him in the afternoon. He flatly refused to face the issue between us.

"Do you have any suggestions for our dealing with

this?" I inquired.

"No."

"Well, perhaps we should postpone the wedding . . . "

The receiver slammed shut in my ear. Silence. I was stunned, then devastated. God had given me other signs in our relationship, and now I had to face the meaning of them.

I climbed into my car and drove to a small nearby lake. The water lapped quietly against the sand, and because it was late in the day, only a handful of people dotted the shore. I wandered aimlessly around the lake, allowing my sunglasses to hide the tears. The ducks drifted in lazy circles on the water, and a small boy sat fishing.

Jim and I had planned to spend the weekend with the Wagners. Dr. Wagner had moved his clinical practice several hundred miles up the California coast, although he still returned to the Foundation for seminars. I decided to visit them alone and called to tell them that plans for the wedding were off.

On Friday I loaded my suitcase into the car and took a stack of tapes to listen to along the way. I had never driven such a long distance—300 miles—in my life. I stopped often to get out and stretch, and to wipe my tears. Glancing in the rearview mirror, I saw the puffy redness that had been so familiar in those last months before Dick's death.

The Wagners greeted me with gentleness and warmth. They didn't pry. Gradually I poured out my grief about this new loss. They sheltered and cared for me, and stood by while I telephoned Bob and Janie to tell them that the wedding was off.

I was not too surprised when both of my children told me they were relieved. Although they had met Jim and liked him well enough, they simply had felt no peace about the wedding, either.

Then I called Dr. Narramore. "I've wrestled and wrestled with this," I explained., "and there will be no wedding and no reception. Could I have my old job back?"

"Jeri," he answered tenderly, "you know you have a job with us as long as you want."

It was hard to return to work. But no one asked any questions. My friends were kind to me, and as time went on, God confirmed again and again that I had made the wise decision. Time put distance between Jim and me, and I began to see clearly that I would have been miserable. Severing our relationship is one of the most difficult things I've ever had to do.

I had thought I needed to be married in order to be happy. Now it was clear that happiness is being in God's will—married or single. Having the right attitude and allowing God to control my life would give me true joy and peace of mind.

It would be dishonest to say that I prefer being single. Of course I would like a partner to share my life. God has given me many friends and has widened my speaking ministry. I am free to travel and enjoy life as a single person. I would be delighted to be married again, but if not, I want to live for God as the very best single person I can.

In the meantime, my sense of worth as an individual has increased. I am a whole person. While it is true that marriage is a mystical union of two people who spiritually unite, it is also true that a single person can be whole.

My identity as a whole person began to come into sharp focus when I realized I was important to God. I didn't have to live in the shadow of a husband in order to have a purpose in life. God has left me here for a purpose, and it is up to me to allow that purpose to find fulfillment.

As a child of God, I have a capacity for unlimited love. As a person who has known both pain and comfort, I have an ability to comfort. My heart has been broken and restored, and therefore I can understand what it means to be wounded and how to offer hope. In many respects, my awareness of my own identity and my recognition of these abilities have come about as a result of the gift of singleness.

Grief Is Not Forever

"It's time you thought about a new one, Mrs. Krumroy," the mechanic said as he slammed the hood of my car. "You've got nearly seventy thousand miles on her. It's been a good one, but nothing lasts forever, you know. I think I've got that oil leak taken care of for now, but it's only a matter of time before you'll have to bring it in again."

I nodded. "Thanks," I said. "I'll give it some thought."

Actually, I'd been trying *not* to think about a new car. Dick had purchased this one for me eight years earlier, just before he died. "Car dealers can spot a widow a mile away," he had said. "I don't want you to get taken."

Before Dick died I had learned to check the oil and to fill the gas tank, and I took a class in simple car care from the auto club. I'd been able to maintain my car with the help of an honest mechanic. Now some of my friends, as well as my mechanic, were advising me to trade for a newer model.

I pulled away from the auto shop and headed for my speaking engagement. "Is it time for me to buy a new car, Lord?" I prayed. "It's a big decision!"

My topic that day was on prayer and praise. I shared with the women the importance of giving thanks to God in all things. When my speech was over, the hostess handed me a bud vase containing two deep purple orchids. In the car, I placed the vase on the seat next to me and headed home.

The vase wobbled and threatened to spill, so I pulled to the side of the quiet neighborhood street and tried to anchor the vase more firmly. Finally it seemed secure, and I turned on the motor and pulled into a driveway to turn around.

The street must have been narrower than I expected. Suddenly I heard a sickening thud. "Oh, no!" I groaned. I climbed out of the car and went back to survey the damage. My fender was crunched into the side of a small pickup truck, and there was no one in sight.

The crash was loud enough to arouse curiosity because two women came out of their front doors.

"Is this your truck?" I asked the woman in red.

"My husband's." She nodded, then put her hand on her chin and shook her head at the other woman.

"I'm so sorry," I said. "Let me give you my driver's license and the name of my insurance company." I wrote the information on my business card and handed it to her. "Do you two know each other?"

The woman in green shook her head. "No, I'm afraid we've never met."

"Are you new in the neighborhood?" I asked.

"We've been here about five years," said the lady in yellow.

"Us, too," the other one offered.

"Do you mean to tell me you've lived here five years and you've never met?" I asked. "I can't believe it! Wait a minute.'

I ran to the front of the car and grabbed the vase. I took the orchids out and handed one to each lady. "Here!" I said. "Let this be the beginning of your friendship!"

I climbed back into the car and drove to the Foundation. My heart was racing, and I felt frustrated. As I drove, I thought about something a friend of mine kept saying to me.

"There's always a way, Jeri. Always an answer. Just because we have a few problems doesn't mean it's the end of the world."

That's true, I reasoned. *The Bible says to praise the Lord in all things. So, Lord, I give praise to you that I can drive. I give praise to you that I'm not struggling with this car on the freeway. I give praise to you that I'm not hurt.*

My friend Jack pulled into the parking lot of the Foundation just after I did.

"Hi, Jeri!" He let out a low whistle. "Ouch! You got

quite a fender bender, there."

I nodded. "Do you think you could follow me over to the car dealer and bring me back?" I asked. "I want to get this repaired."

"Sure. I have an appointment right now, but I'll meet you in an hour."

At the dealership I was shocked to find out that it would take at least three weeks to repair my car. I rented a newer model for the duration. The more I drove it, the more I liked it.

The day I was to pick up my own car, I drove into the dealership and noticed a "For Sale" sign on a demonstration model of the car I had rented. I walked up to the salesman.

"I'm interested in that car," I said.

"Fine." He grinned broadly.

"It's too expensive, though. I'll take it for $2000 less."

He looked at me steadily. "No, I'm afraid we can't lower the price," he said.

"Go ask." I startled myself by my assertiveness.

"Okay, lady, but we just don't do that." He sauntered into the office, and returned a few minutes later, grinning. "Okay, the boss says we can do it."

"Fine. Now I also want trade-in value on my old car that you've just repaired."

He opened his mouth to protest, then thought better of it. "I'll draw up the papers," he said.

"And I want my mechanic to check it out."

He nodded.

The next day I picked the car up and drove it to the service garage. "You got a great deal, here, Mrs. Krumroy," my mechanic said after he'd checked the car. "Who helped you find it?"

"God did." I grinned. I tossed the keys in the air and caught them again. I climbed into my new car and headed toward the Foundation, where I was about to lead another grief seminar. Glancing in the rear view mirror, I smiled at the big brown eyes that stared back at me. Easing out into the traffic, I thought back.

Ten years ago I was so dependent upon Dick that I could never have filled my own gas tank, let alone buy a new car. Dick would hardly know me now. Of course, I'm physically the same—five-foot-two, dark-haired and as trim as I can keep myself. But what a change on the inside! If Dick could see how God had been able to use me since the agony of his death, he'd be delighted.

Ten years ago, I could not have imagined myself spiritually helping anyone. Then, I was a heart-sick wife watching my husband wither before me. It seemed then that the pain would never end, and if it did, I would certainly not want to talk about it.

Yet here I was—no authority, really—ready to tell my story for the thousandth time. Sharing the experience. Shining the light that God had given. Sanctifying the sadness.

I pulled into the parking lot. A little whirlwind tossed a handful of leaves into the air and scattered them across the parking lot. I thought of the first time Dick and I had strolled through the grounds of the Foundation, and of the night he died. I thought of how far my journey had taken me.

God has given me joys and pleasures, friends who come and go, and a satisfying job. With God's love, I have been taught to face the future without resenting the circumstances of the present or the pain of the past. Out of the broken lumber of my deepest sorrow, God has built the foundation for a fuller, richer personality. God has set me on a journey that will enable me to become all that I am intended to be.